THE INDIAN AT COLDITZ

A Novel

RAJAT K. LUTHRA

YODDHA LABS

First published in 2026 by Yoddha Labs

This is a work of fiction inspired by the life of Dr Birendranath Mazumdar (c.1914/15 — December 1997), the only Indian prisoner of war known to have been held at Oflag IV-C, Colditz Castle, during the Second World War.

While certain characters share the names of historical persons, this is a novel, not a biography or a history. All dialogue, interior thoughts, motivations, emotions, relationships, and private conduct depicted in this book are the product of the author's imagination. No dialogue in this novel is a transcript or quotation of any real person's actual words. Certain minor characters are composites, invented for narrative purposes, or amalgamated from multiple historical figures; certain events have been compressed in time, reordered for narrative clarity, or imagined where the historical record is silent. Specific dates, locations, and the broad arc of Dr Mazumdar's wartime service follow the documentary record to the best of the author's research; interpretation, interior life, and dramatic shape are the novelist's own.

The thoughts, feelings, conversations, and private conduct attributed to named individuals are entirely fictional and should not be understood as factual claims about those persons, their character, or their families. Readers seeking the documentary record are directed to the Historical Note at the end of this book.

The author has endeavoured to honour the memory of Dr Mazumdar and of all persons depicted, while exercising the novelist's freedom to imagine what the historical record does not preserve. Any offence to living relatives or descendants of persons named in this novel is unintended and sincerely regretted. Readers who identify factual errors or who have concerns about the depiction of any named person are invited to write to info@yoddhalabs.com; corrections will be considered for subsequent editions.

This novel does not claim to represent the views of any person, family, estate, or institution mentioned within it, including the Imperial War Museum, The National Archives at Kew, the British Army, the Royal Army Medical Corps, the Indian National Army, the estate of Netaji Subhas Chandra Bose, the Colditz Society, or the family and descendants of any person named in this novel. None of these persons, families, estates, or institutions has authorised, endorsed, or reviewed this work.

Typeset in Liberation Serif

ISBN: 978-81-685806-9-5

Cover design by Yoddha Labs

yoddhalabs.com

For my father, who ran out of time.

"Z/240 was very hard to deal with. He disliked being interviewed and expressed the opinion that he was being subjected to treatment that no British POW had to put up with."

— MI5 Assessment, File Z/240
The National Archives, Kew

AUTHOR'S NOTE

The first novel I read as a child was *The Wooden Horse* by Eric Williams, the true story of three men who escaped from a German prison camp by vaulting over a wooden gymnastic horse while other prisoners tunnelled beneath it. I was nine or ten. I read it in a single sitting in my bedroom in New Delhi, and when I finished, I read it again.

After that I could not stop. Paul Brickhill's *The Great Escape*. Pat Reid's *The Colditz Story*. Airey Neave's *They Have Their Exits*. Jack Higgins, Alistair MacLean, and stacks of Commando comics, those palm-sized war stories with their black-and-white panels of tunnels and wire and men doing impossible things behind enemy lines. Between the novels and the comics, the prisoner-of-war escape became the landscape of my imagination. Colditz, in particular, fascinated me: the castle on the rock, the escape committee, the ingenuity, the camaraderie.

But a question nagged at me, even as a boy: where were the Indians?

India contributed two and a half million soldiers to the Allied forces in the Second World War, the largest volunteer army in human history. Indian soldiers were captured across North Africa, Italy, France, and the Far East. Thousands became prisoners of war. And yet, in the vast library of Colditz books and escape literature, I could not find a single Indian face. The shelves were full of English officers tunnelling and disguising and outwitting guards. The millions of Indians who served beside them had been, for the most part, written out of the narrative.

Then, a few years ago, I found him.

Dr Birendranath Mazumdar, a Bengali surgeon, Edinburgh-trained, captured in France in 1940, was the only Indian prisoner of war held at Oflag IV-C, Colditz Castle. He was offered freedom by Subhas Chandra Bose and refused. He conducted a sixteen-day hunger strike. He escaped with a Sikh soldier named Dariao Singh, crawled through wire, and walked nine hundred kilometres across occupied France to Switzerland. After the war, he returned to England, married an Englishwoman named Ruth, and never spoke about what had happened to him. For fifty years.

In 1996, approximately one year before his death, he gave a single oral history recording to the Imperial War Museum (IWM Sound Archive 16245). Ben Macintyre's *Prisoners of the Castle* (Viking, 2022), which draws extensively on that recording, is the authoritative secondary account of Dr Mazumdar's time at Colditz, and this novel's reconstruction of the historical framework relies primarily on Macintyre's research, together with P.R. Reid's Colditz memoirs and records at The National Archives at Kew. The interpretation and interior life presented here are my own imagining.

I did not set out to write a war novel. I set out to answer the question that had nagged me since childhood: did an Indian ever escape from Colditz? The answer was yes, and the man who did it was more extraordinary than any character I could have invented. A doctor who walked toward twenty tanks with a handkerchief. A man who refused the most charismatic revolutionary of his century over fish with mustard. A man who kept his oath for fifty years and could not tell his wife what it had cost him.

This is a novel, not a history. The thoughts, conversations, and interior life of Dr Mazumdar are fiction. The dates, the camps, the escape route, and the arc of his life are, to the best of my research, historically accurate. Where the record was silent, I have imagined. The errors are mine.

The Indian at Colditz is the second publication from Yoddha Labs, following *The Twenty Four* (2026), which told the story of the twenty-four Indian pilots who flew for the RAF during the Second World War. I wrote this book because the boy who read *The Wooden Horse* in his bedroom in New Delhi deserved to know that an Indian was there too.

R.K.L.

New Delhi, 2026

SECTION I

THE WAR

THE HANDKERCHIEF

Chapter 1

The road was straight and the convoy was slow and the countryside on either side had the flat, wet stillness of a place that had recently been fought over and was now waiting to be fought over again.

Forty ambulances. He had counted them that morning at Étaples, counted them as he counted everything, with the automatic precision of a man trained to observe. Forty ambulances carrying five hundred wounded men, the wounded stacked in tiers, the column stretching a quarter-mile along the road to Boulogne and moving at the speed of a man walking, which was slow enough that the hedgerows and the abandoned farmhouses passed with the unhurried progression of a landscape that did not know it was about to end.

May 1940. The roads were choked. Not with military traffic, with everything. Families in horse carts piled with mattresses and kitchen pots. A woman carrying a sewing machine on her back, bent double, the machine's iron treadle swinging with each step. Children who had stopped crying because crying required energy they no longer had. An old man leading a cow. The cow was calm. The cow did not know about the Germans.

He was standing in the lead ambulance with the driver, a corporal from Wolverhampton whose name he had known that morning and would not remember by evening. The road ahead was clear for two hundred yards, then curved left around a copse of trees. Beyond the copse the road continued toward Boulogne. Beyond Boulogne was England.

The tanks came from the trees. Twenty Panzers. They emerged from the copse on the left side of the road the way weather emerges from a horizon, not suddenly but inevitably, the tree line producing them as though the trees had been concealing not tanks but the idea of tanks, the possibility that had been present since the convoy left Étaples and that now resolved itself into steel and noise and the smell of diesel exhaust that would, for the rest of his life, arrive without warning and produce a contraction in his chest that lasted two seconds.

The first shell hit the third ambulance. The sound was not what he expected, a compression rather than an explosion, the air folding inward and then releasing, and the release was the fire. Men inside. He could hear them. The sounds they made were not screams, screams require breath and coordination. These sounds were simpler. The sounds a body makes when it is no longer a body's to make.

Seven seconds later, the seventh ambulance. The convoy stopped. Men were running: drivers, orderlies, walking wounded. Because running was the body's answer to the question the shells were asking and the answer was wrong but the body did not know this.

Boots on the road. He did not remember deciding to get out. The road was soft from rain and his boots sank slightly with each step and he felt this, the mud gripping the soles, the slight resistance, precise, clinical, belonging to the part of his mind that would never stop observing even when the relevant thing was to move.

Heat at twenty yards, not gradually but as a wall, a surface he walked through, and on the other side the air was a different substance, thicker, tasting of petrol and singed hair. He reached into the third ambulance. A hand gripped his wrist. He pulled. The hand belonged to an arm and the arm belonged to a man whose face was not a face, he pulled the man free and laid him on the road and did not look at the face because looking would have cost time.

Three men from the third ambulance. Two from the seventh. He laid them on the verge, on the wet grass, and his hands moved over them with the automatic competence of training: cadavers in London, surgical theatre in Edinburgh, wounded in France. The training held because training was designed to hold.

The tanks had stopped firing. He did not know when, the silence registered retroactively, as pain registers after the injury. The tanks were still there. Twenty of them, arranged in a loose crescent, their turrets pointed at the convoy with the patient certainty of machines that had achieved their purpose.

Silence. He straightened. His shirt was wet: rain, sweat, fluid from the ambulance he did not pause to identify. His hands were black to the wrists. The convoy: forty ambulances, two burning, the drivers crouching behind their doors, the orderlies flat on the ground, the walking wounded in the ditch. No one was moving toward the tanks.

In his pocket, the handkerchief was there, khaki cotton, regulation issue, folded into a square that his fingers found without searching. He unfolded it. He took the baton from under his arm and tied the handkerchief to it. The knot was a reef knot, left over right, right over left, and his fingers made it without trembling: thousands of knots, surgical knots, knots that held arteries shut and skin together, and this was the same knot.

He walked.

Mud gripped his boots. Each step sank and each step required the small effort of extraction, the pulling-free.

Closer now, the tanks. The turrets, the treads, the mud on the undercarriages, the hatches closed, the machine gun barrels tracking him with the slow mechanical patience of instruments that did not know he was a man. He walked toward the lead tank. The handkerchief above his head.

A hatch opened. A man appeared, shoulders first, then head, then hands gripping the turret rim as he pulled himself up and stood on the hull and looked down at the Indian officer walking toward him through the mud with a khaki handkerchief tied to a stick.

The Panzer commander was young. Mid-twenties. Clean-shaven, his uniform pressed. His English was perfect, a native speaker's

English, someone who understood the weight the English placed on courtesy and had adopted it as genuine practice.

He climbed down from the tank. He stood in the road. The mud did not seem to trouble him.

"I'm sorry," he said. His voice was quiet. "I'm afraid you won't reach Boulogne."

Mazumdar stopped. The handkerchief hung from the baton. The two men stood on the road, the German officer and the Indian officer, and between them was the distance that would, for the next seven years, define his life, the distance between a man who has power and a man who has a handkerchief.

"And please," the commander said. "Don't try to escape." Please. The German had said please. Mazumdar heard the word and filed it — in the place that was deeper than memory and more durable than emotion, the place that would hold this word for fifty years and produce it, intact, in a room in Devon when he was old and speaking into a machine that recorded sound, and the word *please* would be among the things he had never said to anyone, this small German courtesy extended on a road in France while the ambulances burned behind him and the war, his war, the war that would cost him everything and give him nothing except the knowledge that he had not broken, began.

They took him. They took the convoy. They took the wounded and the drivers and the dead. They took his baton and his handkerchief and later they would take his sacred thread and his name and replace it with a number.

He walked with the column. The mud had dried on his hands. He could feel it tightening on his skin, the contraction, the stiffness, the thin crust that cracked when he flexed his fingers. He flexed them. The cracking was small and precise and he heard it the way he heard everything: completely, uselessly.

Past hedgerows and fields the column moved, and past the cow, still there, still calm, still eating grass beside the road while the column passed.

He walked. The road was long and the convoy was slow and the countryside on either side had the flat, wet stillness of a place whose future had arrived.

THE MARCH

Chapter 2

His feet went first.

Not gone — ruined. By the second hour the blisters had formed and by the fourth hour the blisters had opened and by the sixth hour the opened blisters had become a fact of walking that the body absorbed — built a room around it, a small interior space where the pain could exist without occupying the whole mind. The road was hard, pressed earth and gravel, the stones sharp beneath the boot soles, each step transmitting the road's surface through leather and sock into the raw skin of the heel. The boots were regulation issue. They had been adequate that morning, were not adequate now, would not be adequate for any of the mornings that followed.

They marched them east. The column was long, two thousand men, perhaps more, the number impossible to count because the column curved with the road, the road with the landscape, flat and featureless, going on. He was near the middle. The men around him were British, infantry, artillery, signals, medical corps, and the men around him did not look at him, they were looking at their feet.

On either side, the Germans marched. Not many. Twenty or thirty, for two thousand prisoners. The prisoners did not need to be guarded in force, the prisoners had nowhere to go. The countryside was German, occupied, patrolled, hostile, and the men who walked through it were defeated men and defeated men do not run. They walk. They put one foot in front of the other and the other in front of the one.

He carried his medical bag. They had not taken it yet. The bag was leather, scuffed, containing instruments he had carried since Edinburgh: stethoscope, scissors, forceps, a tourniquet, gauze, morphine ampules, iodine. The weight of it pulled at his left shoulder — familiar, the familiarity the only thing he possessed that was not the property of the German army.

His left boot had a hole in the sole. The hole had appeared on the second day of marching, and with each step the road came through the hole and pressed against his sock.

Men fell. They fell without announcement, the legs simply stopping, the body folding, the road receiving them. The guards did not stop the column. They pulled the fallen men to the side and left them, or pulled them up and pushed them back into line. The pulling-up was logistics, not kindness; a man on the road was an obstacle and obstacles slowed the column.

Three men in the first hour he treated. Two with heat exhaustion, one with a laceration across his palm where he had fallen on a stone. He treated them while walking, the bag open, the hands working, the instruments finding what they needed, trained to find what they needed, the training requiring no permission from the Germans or the road or the war.

A corporal from the Suffolks walked beside him for a mile. The corporal was limping badly and Mazumdar looked at the limp and said, "Take your left boot off."

The corporal stared at him. "Your left boot. Take it off. The blister is between the third and fourth metatarsals and you are compensating by pronating, which is making it worse."

The corporal took his boot off. The blister was between the third and fourth metatarsals. Mazumdar drained it with a needle from his bag, applied iodine, cut a piece of gauze and folded it into a pad and placed it between the toes.

"Keep the pad there. It will take the pressure off the head."

The corporal looked at him: at the brown face beneath the officer's cap, at the medical bag, at the hands that had just done what no other man in the column could do. The corporal's expression was not gratitude. It was confusion, helped by a person he could not place in the categories the army had given him.

"Thank you, sir." Sir. The corporal had seen the pips. The pips were what the pips were: rank, authority, the King's Commission. The corporal had responded to the pips before he had responded to the face. The corporal would remember the pips. He would not remember the face.

After the corporal, the column continued. They walked through villages that had been emptied. Shuttered windows. A dog tied to a post, barking until the column passed and then barking at the silence the column left behind. The smell of smoke from a house that had burned days ago and was still smouldering, no one left to put it out.

Thirst arrived in the third hour. The Germans had not offered water. The prisoners drank from ditches when the column slowed, kneeling at the road's edge and cupping the water in their hands. He drank. The water was cold and brown, tasted of earth and minerals; he felt it travel his oesophagus and arrive in his stomach with disproportionate attention to the act.

Night came. They marched in the dark. The sound of two thousand pairs of boots on a road that was no longer visible, rhythmic, impersonal, a machine that did not care who was inside it. They slept in a field. No shelter. The ground was damp and the cold came through his uniform and reached his skin within minutes. He slept two hours, maybe three. His body woke because bodies wake when the ground is cold and the mind has not yet learned to suppress the instincts it will learn to suppress. He urinated at the edge of the field. A guard turned his torch toward the sound. The light found him, an Indian officer in a French field at four in the morning, and the light stayed on him for three seconds and moved on.

By dawn the second day was already worse. The blisters had deepened past the dermis. Men who had limped yesterday were being carried. Men who had been carried were being left. The arithmetic of a forced march, the column moves at the pace the guards set and the men who cannot maintain the pace are subtracted and the subtraction is permanent.

Outside a village with no sign he passed a man sitting at the road's edge. A sergeant, the Hampshires, judging by the badge. The sergeant's boots were off, his feet in his hands, the feet the colour of meat that has been left out and the sergeant was looking at them with the expression of a man examining an injury he could not reverse. Mazumdar slowed. The sergeant looked up. Their eyes met. Mazumdar could see the diagnosis, cellulitis, possibly early gangrene, certainly immobile, and the sergeant could see that Mazumdar could see the diagnosis. Neither of them spoke. The column moved. Mazumdar moved with it.

He kept pace. His legs worked. His lungs worked. His heart, when he checked it, fingers on the radial artery, the count automatic, was seventy-eight beats per minute. Elevated. Not dangerous.

Around him, the noticing. Not all of them, most were too deep in their own suffering to notice anything beyond the back of the man in front of them. But some noticed. He could feel it, a small pressure at the back of the neck, a shift in the air's temperature. An Indian. In a British uniform. Walking beside them through France as a prisoner of the Germans. The noticing was neither hostile nor friendly, the attention paid to a thing that does not fit the pattern.

No one spoke to him about it. No one asked where he was from or how he had come to be here or what an Indian was doing in the Royal Army Medical Corps.

The third day they reached Nijmegen.

The barges were worse.

Nijmegen. Three days of marching. They reached a canal. On the canal were barges, coal barges, low in the water, open-topped, black with the residue of the coal they had carried and would carry again when the cargo of men had been delivered. The men were loaded in. Packed. Standing first, then sitting, then pressed into a density that eliminated posture and left only contact: shoulders, knees, elbows, the back of a stranger's head against his chest, the smell of a stranger's sweat in his mouth.

Slow on the canal, the barge. The canal was narrow and the sky above it was a rectangle, the canal banks on either side, the sky between them, a strip of grey that was the only openness available to men who were enclosed on every other side. He looked up. The rectangle moved as the barge moved, the slow passage of trees and bridges, the occasional face of a Dutch civilian watching from a towpath with an expression that contained pity and relief and the look of a person watching suffering from which they have been spared.

He stood for the first six hours. His knees locked. His back ached. The men around him shifted, hydraulic, the barge tilted and the bodies moved, the bodies moved the other bodies, continuous and small and exhausting. A man beside him vomited. The vomit ran between their boots. Neither of them could move away from it. The man apologised, a lance corporal, young, his face grey, his eyes communicating the shame of a body that has lost control of itself in the proximity of strangers. Mazumdar said nothing.

What he would remember was the smell. The coal residue and the men, the canal water and the sweetness of dysentery, he identified it within the first hour, the smell unmistakable, the men who had it unable to move to the barge's edge and the men around them unable to move away. The excrement was on the deck within hours. It mixed with the coal dust, the canal water that sloshed through the hull. The mixture was black. The men stood in it. The standing was war.

The river. The canal opened, briefly, into a wider waterway, a river, grey-brown, the current visible in the patterns on the surface. The barge slowed in the current. Bodies pressed closer. The water was beneath him and the bodies were around him and the smell of the river came through the other smells, the mineral smell of moving water, and —

The Ganges. The ghats at Varanasi. His father's hand on his shoulder, the boy standing at the top of the steps while the dawn light turned the water to copper and the bodies of the bathers were waist-deep and the sound was the opposite of silence, a thousand voices murmuring prayers that merged into a single sound that was the river's own voice.

Three seconds. Then the barge lurched and a man's elbow hit his ribs, the Ganges was gone and the canal was back and the bodies around him were not bathers and the water beneath him was not sacred and the smell was excrement and coal and the bodies of men who had not washed in four days.

Then Kassel.

THE HEAD

Chapter 3

I

Kassel was a processing camp. The word *processing* was the German word and the word meant what it meant in every institution he had known, the reduction of a person to a series of administrative acts performed on his body, his belongings, and his name, the acts proceeding in an order that had been determined before his arrival and that would proceed in the same order for the man behind him and the man behind that man.

They lined up in the yard. The yard was concrete, clean in a way that the road and the barge had not been clean. He stood in the line and waited.

In front of him, a lieutenant, Royal Artillery, whose hands were shaking. Bilateral fine tremor, not cold, the adrenal signature, the body outpacing composure.

One at a time, they were called forward. A table. Two German officers, one seated, one standing. The seated officer had a ledger. The standing officer had a box.

II

"Name."

"Captain Birendranath Mazumdar. Royal Army Medical Corps."

A pen stopped. The seated officer looked up, a small disruption in the rhythm of the processing, the officer had been writing names for hours and the name he had just heard did not fit the hand's expectation.

"Again." "Birendranath Mazumdar. M-A-Z-U-M-D-A-R." A pen scratched the ledger. The name was in. "Your belongings. On the table." On the table: the gold cigarette case, a gift from a colleague in Edinburgh, engraved with his initials, the metal warm from his pocket. The lighter. The Parker pen, black with a gold clip, the nib worn to his hand's pressure, the pen he had used for letters, for case notes, for the prescriptions that bore his signature. The pencil. The typewriter: portable, Remington, carried in its case from London to France. Each object on the table was a subtraction.

Into the box, each item. The placing was methodical. The box filled.

"Medical bag." Beside his left foot, the bag. The bag had been there for four days and two nights and six years before that. The stethoscope was in the bag. The stethoscope had been in every room he had entered as a physician, the wards in Edinburgh, the consulting rooms in London, the field hospital at Étaples, the road where the ambulances burned. The stethoscope was not a possession. It was a faculty, like hearing, like sight.

"The medical bag." On the table. The officer placed it in the box. The officer closed the box.

III

Tiled, cold, smelling of carbolic and the chemical sweetness of the powder they used, the delousing room. Men stripped. Uniforms taken, placed in bags, marked with numbers. The tile was cold under bare feet. His eye moved over the stripped men involuntarily, the variations in muscle wasting, the bruising at different stages of resolution, a clavicle set badly. The sound of the room was breathing, the shuffle of men moving where they were told to move. The dusting, the powder hitting skin with a soft percussion, shoulders and arms and groin, and the chemical sting reaching the nostrils before the powder reached the skin.

Layer by layer the uniform came off: shirt, trousers, tunic, the fabric stiff with four days of sweat and road dirt and coal dust. The cigarette case was gone. The pen was gone. The stethoscope was gone. Now the uniform. Without it he was a man in underclothes standing on tile.

Left shoulder to right hip, the sacred thread. Cotton. Thin — a twist of three threads, white once, now the colour of skin, the colour of cloth worn so long it has become the body. He had received it at the Upanayana. He had been eleven. His father had placed it over his left shoulder. The placing had been the moment. Not the prayers before, not the fasting, not the fire, not the priest's Sanskrit — his father's hands lifted the thread and settled it across his son's body, a transference, the father giving the son entry into a lineage that extended backward beyond memory and forward beyond death and the thread was the physical fact of this lineage, worn against the skin, slept in, bathed in, never removed.

A large hand, reddened from handling bodies all day, the German orderly reached for it. He saw the hand coming and the hand closed on the thread and pulled.

"Was ist das?" He did not answer quickly enough. The thread was thin. The hand was strong. The thread broke. The orderly held it, a short length of dirty cotton, meaningless, a piece of string. He looked at it, looked at him, dropped it on the floor, the indifference of a man disposing of a thing that was not on the inventory and therefore did not exist.

The thread lay on the tile. He looked at it. He could have picked it up. The orderly had moved to the next man. The thread was on the floor and his feet were on the floor, the distance between them was eighteen inches and the picking-up would have taken two seconds. He did not pick it up.

Cold on his skin, the chemical powder. They dusted him. Arms raised, legs apart, the powder settling into the hair on his chest and his arms and his groin. Thorough. Impersonal.

IV

In the next room, the barber.

Hair on the floor: blond, brown, auburn, red, the hair of the men who had sat in the chair before him, mixed and indistinguishable.

"Sit." He sat. The clippers buzzed. The barber, a German private, young, bored after six hours of cutting hair, placed his hand on the top of Mazumdar's head and tilted it forward. The hand was firm. The clippers approached his temple.

An officer entered. Older, a captain. He looked at Mazumdar. Not administrative, not cursory, assessment.

"This one is not European," the officer said, in German. Mazumdar understood the German. "Full shave. Delousing protocol for non-Europeans."

The barber adjusted the clippers. The blade guard came off.

"No." He said it in English. The word was clear and the word was quiet and the word stopped the barber's hand.

"You only shave your head when your father or mother dies. I am not going to shave my head under any condition."

Both men stared, the officer, the barber. The room held still.

"You will comply." "I will not." His father was alive. His father was in a house in Gaya where the mango tree grew in the courtyard and the morning surgery began at eight, between the surgeries his father sat in the chair where the light was best and read *The Times*, the imported copy, days old by the time it arrived, the news already history. His father was alive and the shaving of the head was a death rite, the son's head shaved at the father's cremation, the hair offered, the grief made visible on the body, and to shave the head when the father lived was to perform the ritual in advance, to announce a death that had not occurred, to invite by gesture the thing the gesture mourned.

He did not comply. German, then English, then German again, the shouting filled the room. Two guards were called. The guards took his arms. He did not resist physically, the arms were held, and the resistance was in the word, the single word, *no*, spoken once and not repeated because repetition would have been negotiation and he was not negotiating.

They took him to the barber by force. The clippers touched his temple. He twisted his head. The clippers cut a line across his scalp, a stripe, a furrow, the hair falling in a dark comma on the tile, and the German officer assessed the calculation in the time it took the clippers to cut the second stripe and stopped. Visibility meant witnesses. Witnesses meant a report.

"Solitary."

V

Stone walls, stone floor, a wooden bench, a bucket. No window. A slot in the door through which light entered as a line: horizontal, thin, the width of a hand, dividing the dark into above and below.

He sat on the bench. His head was partially shaved, the two stripes raw and exposed, the rest of his hair intact. He touched the stripes. The skin was rough where the blade had passed, the stubble already beginning.

Cold came through the wood of the bench into his thighs and through the stone of the wall into his back. Stone cold, the cold of a material that absorbs heat from everything that touches it and returns nothing.

No clock. The line of light from the slot did not change, the corridor beyond was lit by electricity, not by sun, and electricity knows nothing about time. He sat. The dark surrounded him. He had been in dark rooms before, the surgery at night when the kerosene ran low, the ship's cabin crossing to England, the ambulance on the road to Boulogne. Those darks had been temporary. This dark was built for the purpose of containing a man in the absence of light.

His father's face. His father's hands, the hands in the surgery, the hands on the table at dinner, the hands that had held the thread at the Upanayana and placed it over his shoulder with a steadiness that came from certainty rather than ceremony. A man performing an act he believed in completely. The thread connected the boy to a lineage older than the boy, older than the house, older than the country. The connection was not metaphor but cotton, three threads of raw cotton twisted, worn against the skin. That cotton was now on a tile floor in a room two corridors away.

He sat in the dark with this. Dark held everything. The thread on the floor. The stripes on his head. The cigarette case in a box, the stethoscope in a box, the name in a ledger. The road, the barge, the column, the handkerchief, the Panzer commander who had said *please*.

He lay on the bench. The wood was hard. The cold unchanged. He closed his eyes but it made no difference. The first night was long.

VI

Morning, or what he was told was morning. The corridor unchanged, the light from the slot unchanged, the only evidence was the guard's face and the guard's gesture toward the open door.

Brightness. The sun was low and after the dark the brightness was a pain behind his eyes, the pupils constricting, the adjustment involuntary, the iris performing the one function the cell had not been able to suppress.

Some of the other prisoners looked at him. The ones who looked saw the stripes, the two raw lines where the clippers had cut and the rest of the hair untouched.

He touched his head. The stubble was sharp. They issued him a uniform. German: grey, coarse, the fabric heavy and unfamiliar, the cut designed for a different body. They issued him a number. The number replaced the name.

Bread: dense, dark, the texture of compressed grain. A tin of meat he did not open. A tin cup of liquid that was called coffee and that tasted of nothing he could identify as coffee. He ate the bread. He held it in his hands. Heavy. The first German food.

THE OTHER INDIANS

Chapter 4

I

The Kommandant's office smelled of floor polish and cigarettes and the smell was deliberate and precise. The floor was clean. The desk was clean. The windows were clean, the cleanness had a smell he recognised from surgical theatres, the carbolic absence of the organic, every surface scrubbed of evidence of any human occupation. After three weeks at Kassel, the yard, the cell, the delousing room, the barracks that smelled of men and damp wool, the cleanness.

Two men waited for him. A German officer, completely bald, the baldness giving his head a polished, institutional look, a surface designed to communicate authority without ornament. And a young Indian.

Civilian clothes, a suit, pressed, the jacket slightly too large for the man inside it. The man was twenty-five, or near it. His face was smooth and his eyes were careful and his hands were folded in his lap, deliberate, hands arranged for performance.

Mazumdar stood. They had not offered him a chair. German first, then English, the bald officer spoke with the accent heavy, the words chosen with the care of a man delivering a prepared text. "You are an

Indian. Captain Mazumdar. You are a King's Commissioned Officer in the British Army. An officer of considerable standing."

"The British are not your people. They occupy your country. They tax your people. They deny your people self-governance. You know this. You are an educated man."

"We are offering you a good life. A comfortable life. All you must do is make a broadcast, a radio broadcast, encouraging your countrymen to join the Indian Legion. To fight for their own freedom. You would be speaking the truth. You would be serving India."

The young Indian leaned forward. He produced photographs, black and white, glossy, the paper smooth. London. The photographs showed London burning. The Blitz. Buildings Mazumdar knew, streets he had walked, the hospital where he had trained, the terraces where he had lived, the buildings broken, the roofs gone, the interiors exposed like wounds. The young man's voice was soft. "The war is virtually over. Germany has won. It is foolish to endure the hardships of a prisoner when you could be living in comfort and freedom."

Between them on the desk, the photographs. London in ruins. The anatomy hall where he had opened his first cadaver, the building might be rubble. The landlady's house in Bloomsbury where he had rented a room. The landlady had hesitated at the door, her hand on the latch. The hesitation had lasted two seconds and contained everything — the brown face, the medical bag, the accent that was educated but not English. Resolved in his favour, yet the hesitation remained, and the hesitation was London, and London was burning in the photographs on the desk.

"I cannot do it."

The bald officer's expression did not change. The young Indian's expression did not change. The photographs remained on the desk. Mazumdar was marched out.

II

The camps were the same camp.

Kassel. Then another, the name forgotten within days, the wire the same wire, the barracks the same barracks. Then another. Then another. Twelve camps in sixteen months, a recurring presentation, same symptoms, different ward. The transfers came without warning. A guard at the door. Pack your things. The things were nothing, a change of clothes, a blanket whose wool had thinned to gauze, the notebook he had begun filling with Bengali script. The packing took two minutes. The walking to the truck took five. The truck took hours.

At each camp the same sequence. Registration. Number confirmed. Barracks assigned. Bunk allocated, always the worst bunk, the one nearest the door or farthest from the stove, the choice determined by some calculus of unwantedness. The forms had no box for him. The system processed white officers, their ranks, their regiments, their next of kin in Hampshire and Kent, and when an Indian doctor arrived the system paused, confused, recalculated, and assigned him to the nearest approximation, which was no approximation at all.

At one camp, the name began with L, or possibly M, a British officer asked him to examine a wound on his leg. Mazumdar examined it. The wound was infected, cellulitis tracking along the anterior tibial, the smell already present, the trajectory clear. He cleaned it with what he had and dressed it with what he could find, told the officer to keep the leg elevated and to request antibiotics from the camp doctor. The officer thanked him and did not speak to him again. The wound healed. Two weeks later the officer walked without a limp. The officer walked past him without recognition.

At another camp a guard brought him a letter. The letter was from the Red Cross, addressed to his name, confirming his status as a prisoner of war. He held it, the paper, the official stamp, the typed words, the first time in months that he had held a document that acknowledged his existence by name rather than by number. He kept the letter in his notebook.

Monthly, the Red Cross parcels arrived. The distribution followed the networks of school, regiment, accent. The networks did not include him. He watched the tins being opened and the chocolate being broken into squares, the squares being passed from hand to hand and the hands did not pass to him.

"They had the food but they wouldn't share it," he would say, fifty years later, into a machine. "These were so-called educated people. I couldn't believe my eyes."

He did not say this at the time. At the time he said nothing. He ate what he was given.

The German rations were dark bread and thin soup and whatever meat came, horsemeat, the taste uncertain. He ate them. The bread was heavy and stayed in the stomach longer than soft bread, and the staying was useful, the body rationing what little energy the calories provided.

Worse in a different way, the Germans. At Kassel they had tried persuasion. At the intermediate camps they tried contempt. "You are an Indian. Why should you care if a few Tommies die?"

At one camp he stood in the dispensary doorway until the camp doctor looked up. The doctor was grey, hair grey, the skin grey where the day had not reached it. He held a fountain pen with the precision of a man for whom instruments were obedience. When he looked up his eyes moved first and the rest of his face followed, delayed, as if the apparatus of expression operated on separate circuits. He was fifty, or looked it. The uniform was pressed. The desk was empty.

"The men in Barracks Four have scurvy," Mazumdar said. He said it in German. The camp doctor did not move. "Skorbutus. Vitamin C deficiency." The Latin was better, the only language where they met as colleagues, if colleagues was what he was proposing. "Vitaminosis C deficientia. The symptoms are in the mouth, I can show you, if you are unfamiliar."

The camp doctor's hand shifted. The pen remained in the hand. The fingers did not release it.

"They have bleeding gums. Gingival haemorrhage. The teeth are loose, spontaneous dentition loss." Mazumdar heard the precision in his own voice, the clinical tone that was a shield and a weapon both. "There is bruising on the legs, petechial eruption along the anterior tibial surface. Ecchymoses. The skin has begun to bleed from within. Without supplementation, the collagen synthesis fails. The healed wounds open. The gums become necrotic. The men will lose their teeth and then their lives."

The camp doctor stared. His eyes had not moved. The pen had not moved. The expression on his face was the expression of a man being lectured by what he had chosen not to see, a prisoner, a brown man, a shadow that had moved from the periphery to occupy the space where a doctor should stand. The expression was anger beneath the surface, so thoroughly suppressed that it appeared as absence, as the deliberate refusal of any gesture at all.

"The trajectory is rapid. One month. Two. Vitamin C absorption has already failed. The men are depleting their reserves." Mazumdar stopped. He had been speaking for longer than was useful. The sound of his own voice had begun to sound like pleading. He did not plead.

"You will leave," the camp doctor said. His accent was perfect. His voice was soft.

Mazumdar left. He walked down the dispensary corridor and the door closed behind him, sealed, with the exact weight of the frame against its catch. His hand held the medical bag. It was the bag the Germans had issued, inferior to the one he had carried in Edinburgh, the leather already cracking. But it was a bag. He walked with it down the corridor and into the yard where the wire ran grey against the sky and the men were moving slowly through their routines, the movements of men with bleeding gums, the movements of men who were dying one tooth at a time.

Each complaint was noted. Each transfer was, in part, a response.

In August, between transfers, the news reached him. Tagore was dead. Rabindranath Tagore, the man who had given Bengal its language. Dead on August 7, in Calcutta, while a Bengali sat in a German camp. He sat on his bunk that evening and opened the notebook and the notebook was already half full of Bengali words.

III

Marienberg. Summer, 1941.

On a hillside, the camp. The wire ran along a ridge and below the ridge a second compound held Russian prisoners, Soviet soldiers captured on the Eastern Front, men for whom the Geneva Convention did not apply because the Soviet Union had not signed it.

Through the wire he could see them. Every day from the yard where he walked, the Russian compound below, the men in it thin beyond short rations — starvation. They moved slowly. Some did not move. The ones who did not move were carried by the ones who did and sometimes the man being carried had stopped needing to be carried, and this was visible from the ridge.

They reached through the wire. Hands. Thin hands, the fingers extended, the gesture universal. They were asking for food. They were asking for medicine. They were asking in Russian, which he did not speak, and the not-speaking did not matter because the hands spoke.

He was a doctor. The hands could see the medical bag — they had given him a new one at Kassel, a German bag, inferior, but a bag, and the hands recognised it. He stood at the wire on his side and they stood at the wire on theirs, between the two wires was a strip of earth that belonged to no one and the strip was ten feet wide and the ten feet were uncrossable.

From where he stood he could diagnose. Dysentery, the gait, the staining on the trousers. Typhus, the flush, the tremor. Tuberculosis, the cough that carried across the wire. Scurvy, the bruising visible even at distance. He could diagnose and he could not treat. The surgeon's hands idle. The surgeon's eyes working.

His father's hands. The memory arrived without announcement: Gaya, June, the riverbed white and dry, the children crossing it as though it were a road. His father pressed a palm to the sand. *Here, Biren. Below.* Something moved beneath the crust, felt through the skin but not visible from above, present and invisible, giving no sign to anyone who had not been shown where to press.

Edinburgh surfaced, the anatomy hall. His first cadaver. The body on the table, the skin grey, the smell of formaldehyde so strong it lived in his clothes for weeks. The professor, MacGregor, a Scot, precise, who had looked at him on the first day and said: “Mr Mazumdar, you will take the left thorax.” Not a question. Not a concession. An assignment.

IV

A second recruitment, at Marienberg. A young German officer, different from the first. “Have you changed your mind? Will you speak on the wireless?”

“No.” “Will you at least go to Berlin?” He shook his head. “Well, you are going anyway.” He asked for an orderly. He was an officer. Officers were entitled to an orderly to carry their luggage. The German officer did not find this amusing. Two soldiers with revolvers marched him to the train. He carried his own suitcase.

Berlin. An office block. The same bald officer from Kassel and another, more senior. “Have you changed your mind about making a broadcast?”

“No. And what is more, you are ascribing to me an importance that I do not possess, and do not even claim.”

The senior officer changed his approach. “When were you last with a woman?”

“If you think my honour can be bought with a woman, you are very wrong.”

The senior officer turned to the bald officer. “This man is *deutschfeindlich*.” Anti-German.

“Well,” Mazumdar said. “You are the best judges of that.” They sent him to Colditz.

THE CASTLE

Chapter 5

The castle was on a rock.

From the truck he saw it — through the canvas flap, the road climbing, the headlights sweeping the trees and then the trees ending and the rock beginning. The rock was massive. The castle sat on it as if it had always been there, the stone of the castle continuous with the stone of the cliff, as though the building had been extracted from the geology beneath it. It rose in the dark, bathed in searchlights, the beams white against the yellow-grey walls, the towers dark, the windows dark, the whole structure emerging from the rock like a plate from a Gothic novel.

September 26, 1941. The truck stopped. The gate was enormous: iron, studded, built for a century that understood what gates were for. The gate opened. The truck passed through. The gate closed.

Cobblestones. The courtyard was lit by a single lamp and the lamp made the cobblestones shine, the only movement, because everything else was still. Stone walls on three sides. A chapel on the fourth. The sky above, a rectangle, darker than the walls, the stars visible through the gap the walls made. He had seen this rectangle before. On the barge. On the canal. The sky reduced to the shape the walls permitted.

His boots hit the cobblestones and the sound was loud, the courtyard amplifying every sound, designed to amplify, to listen, to hold the sounds of the men inside it as a bowl holds water.

No one was in the courtyard. The prisoners were in their quarters. Past midnight, the transport timed for this, a man arriving in a place he cannot see, the building larger than the darkness that contains it.

In the courtyard he stood. A sentry was in the gatehouse, visible through the window, the shape of a man in a chair, the orange point of a cigarette. Mazumdar walked to the gatehouse window. The sentry looked up.

"Wo bin ich?" Where am I? The sentry looked at him. The looking lasted several seconds, long enough for the sentry to register the face, the uniform, the brown skin, the fact that the new arrival was speaking German with a fluency the sentry had not expected from a man who looked like this man looked. The sentry did not answer. He put his finger to his lips. The cigarette glowed.

They left him in the dark. A guard came eventually, ten or twenty minutes, the time unmeasurable in a courtyard with no clock. The guard led him through a door and up stairs, stone stairs, narrow, turning, the walls close on either side, the ceiling low enough that he had to lower his head at the turns. His calves burned on the third flight, the march still in the muscles, the weeks at Kassel still in the joints, the body's ledger open and accounting. Up. Past a landing. Up again. Past another. The castle went up, each flight of stairs adding distance between him and the courtyard, the gate, the ground.

The attic. A long room under the eaves. The ceiling sloped. Wooden beams crossed above, dark with age. The room smelled of wool and men and the cold that lives in the highest rooms of old buildings, the cold that rises, that is always there, that the heating below does not reach because the heating was not designed for the room where the least important people sleep.

Bunks. Three tiers. Men asleep, the breathing and the shifting and the small sounds of men who have learned to sleep in proximity. A wheeze from the second tier, left side, bronchial, the pitch too high for fluid. A man two bunks down breathed through his mouth, the nasal obstruction audible, chronic, untreated. The guard pointed. Top bunk.

Back of the room. Farthest from the door, the stove, the single window, the other men. The point farthest from everything.

Into the bunk he climbed. The mattress was thin. The blanket was wool and not sufficient. He lay on his back. Somewhere below, a key turned in a lock. The click was small and precise, it entered the room and entered him — not the gate or the courtyard or the stairs but this, the click of a key in a lock in the dark, the sound that said the building had him now.

He was, to say the least, miserable and lost. His words. He would use them later, decades later, speaking into a tape recorder in a room in Devon with careful understatement — fifty years compressing this moment into a sentence. *Miserable and lost.*

Eighteen inches above him, the ceiling. The wooden beams were dark and the grain was visible even in the faint light from the window, the grain ran in lines that curved and converged, a surface that had been looked at by every man who had ever lain in this bunk. He looked at it. There was nothing else.

The ceiling of his room in Gaya had been white. Plaster, cracked in the corner where the monsoon damp came through each year, the crack repaired and re-cracked in a cycle his mother called the house breathing. The crack was shaped like a river.

Below, in the rooms beneath the attic, sounds, muffled, distant. A door closing. A voice. Laughter. Men who belonged to each other, who shared a room and a language, a war and a joke he would not hear the punchline of.

Two o'clock. The sound came from somewhere beyond the walls, a bell, deep, the vibration carrying through the stone. For one man in the uppermost bunk in the uppermost room the sound was the first measure of a time that would be measured in this way: by bells, by Appell, by the rectangle of sky changing from grey to blue to grey, for the next seventeen months.

He was the only Indian. Wool scratched his neck where the blanket met his chin. The ceiling was close. The beams were dark. Below, the laughter had stopped. The clock did not strike again. The silence was the castle. The castle held him. The understanding lived in the dark above the bunk, the beams, the wool, the cold, the sleeping men who did not know he was here and would, in the morning, look at him and see a face they had not expected to see and the seeing would be the beginning of a different kind of war.

A bell woke him. Not the church clock, a different bell, sharper, closer. The attic stirred. Men moved in their bunks, blankets pushed back, feet hitting the wooden floor, the groaning of men woken by a sound they despise and cannot refuse.

Down from the bunk. His ankles protested: stiff from the cold, the plantar fascia tight, the first steps of the morning requiring negotiation. The men around him were white. Every man who glanced at him as he climbed down from the top bunk at the back of the room was white, the first event of his first morning at Colditz, a series of faces turning toward him and turning away.

One man held the glance. Red-haired, tall, standing by the window with his braces over his shoulders. The man's face performed a small calculation, the brown skin, the uniform, the bunk assignment, and the calculation produced nothing. Not hostility. Not welcome. A blankness. He turned to the man beside him and said a word Mazumdar did not hear and the man beside him looked.

Down the stairs and into the courtyard. The courtyard in daylight, the rectangle of cobblestones, the walls rising on three sides, the chapel, the sky above grey with the specific grey of Saxony in autumn. The walls were higher than he had understood.

A man approached him. Older, moustached, the bearing of authority carried in the shoulders and the jaw. This was the Senior British Officer, Colonel Guy Dorian, who had been captured in France and transferred to Colditz for a persistent refusal to cooperate with his captors, and who now ran the British contingent with rigid propriety.

"You there." Mazumdar stopped. He was standing in the courtyard in the uniform he had been captured in, creased and thin and bearing the markings of a rank he had earned in a recruiting office in another country in another year. He had not saluted.

"You're still in the King's army," Dorian said. The sentence was delivered without warmth or malice, a correction, the colonel informing the new arrival that the castle did not suspend the regulations the army had built. He saluted.

Dorian looked at him. The look was brief, comprehensive, the officer's habit of reading a man in three seconds: rank, condition, usefulness. What he saw, a brown officer, five foot seven, compact across the shoulders, the posture upright but the uniform hanging where the body had shrunk beneath it. The voice, when it came, was quiet and precise and carried the vowels of an English education. The face was watchful. The brown face entered the assessment. The assessment was filed.

Mazumdar read him back. The facial plethora, the capillary dilation across the nose and cheeks, the resting respiratory rate slightly elevated for a man standing still. The colonel's liver was working harder than the colonel knew.

I was not impressed, Mazumdar would say later. *I disliked him at once.*

He stood at the margin because the margin was where he stood, the beginning.

THE SYSTEM

Chapter 6

I

The days were identical. This was the first thing to understand about Colditz and the last thing you stopped noticing. Appell at seven, the courtyard, the counting, the German NCO moving down the rows with his clipboard while the officers stood in whatever formation resentment and half-sleep produced. Then breakfast. Then the courtyard. Then lunch. Then the courtyard. Then Appell again at four. Then the hours until dark. Then the dark.

Twenty-seven metres on three sides, the walls rose, and higher on the fourth where the chapel abutted the Kommandantur. The sky above was a rectangle too, grey mostly, or white, or the pale blue of a Saxon winter that looked like colour had been removed from it. The men walked in it. They walked in circles or in lines or in the aimless diagonal patterns of men who had nowhere to arrive. Mazumdar walked at the margins. He had found, within the first week, that the margins were where he would walk, because the centre of the courtyard belonged to the groups and the groups had formed without him.

There were the public school men, Etonians, Harrovians, Wykehamists, who moved through the castle with the easy confidence of people for whom institutional confinement was not entirely unfamiliar, merely less comfortable than the version they had chosen. There were the grammar school officers, who occupied the next stratum and who aped the manners of the first without the accent. There were the colonials, Australians, New Zealanders, South Africans, who held themselves apart with a different kind of ease, looser, more physical, less deferential. There were the French in their own quarters and the Dutch in theirs and the Poles who kept to themselves with a ferocity that suggested they had learned, before the British, that no one else could be trusted.

And there was Mazumdar. He did not occupy a stratum. He occupied a position outside all strata, not at the bottom of the hierarchy but beyond it. The men did not exclude him by decision. No memorandum was circulated. No meeting was held. The exclusion was a shift in posture when he approached a group, a conversation that did not pause but changed register, a seat at the dining table that was technically available and practically uninhabitable. The chair near the draught. The bunk at the back of the attic. The portion served last.

Top bunk, uppermost attic, the farthest from the stove, the closest to the roof, the coldest position in the building. He climbed to it each night on iron rungs that rang beneath his hands. The metal held the temperature of the stone — seven degrees, he estimated, possibly six; his fingertips had lost peripheral sensation by the third rung. The ceiling above was low enough that he could not sit upright. The window showed a strip of sky that changed colour with the season and temperature with the hour. He watched it, the only privacy the castle permitted. Pigeons nested in the eaves. He could hear them through the wall, the low, persistent sound of creatures that had chosen to live inside a building that no one else had chosen.

At night the attic belonged to the sounds the men could not prevent, the coughing, the shifting, the creaking of iron bunks adjusting to the weight of bodies that could not adjust to them. And the clogs. His bladder woke him at two or three in the morning. Crossing the attic floor in the dark required wooden clogs. The clogs clattered on the stone and the clattering woke men who did not want to be woken and the voice that came from the dark — "What the hell is the matter with you, Mazumdar?" — was the voice of a building in which his body was an inconvenience even when it performed the most basic of functions.

II

They called him Jumbo.

He did not know, at first, what the name meant. He heard it in the courtyard, in the mess, in the corridor outside the washroom, called out with the forced cheer the British use when they wish to pretend that cruelty is affection. "Morning, Jumbo." "Coming through, Jumbo." Jumbo was an elephant, a Victorian circus elephant, famous, caged, transported from one exhibition to another for the entertainment of crowds. *Loxodonta africana*, African, not Indian, a distinction any naturalist would make and no one at Colditz had bothered to. The misclassification was the point.

Unable to shift the name, he tried introducing himself with his rank, his title, his surname, and found that the castle had decided for him, as it decided everything, by consensus so quiet it resembled nature. To object was to confirm the designation. To ignore it was to accept it. He chose a third option: he heard it, and each time he felt the small contraction at the back of his jaw, the masseter tightening, a quarter-millimetre of clenching, involuntary and invisible. He allowed the jaw its knowledge and denied it expression.

The jaw tightened again in the kitchen. The kitchen was cold and stone-floored, reeking of boiled cabbage and food cooked in insufficient fat. The ventilation was wrong, a single high window, steam condensing on stone, the air pooling at floor level where the temperature differential trapped it. The British officers had decided that Mazumdar could make curry. He was Indian. Indians made curry. The logic was total, unassailable. It bore no relationship to the fact that he had seldom cooked a meal in his life, that his mother's kitchen in

Gaya had been a kingdom he was not permitted to enter, that the smell of mustard oil heating in an iron kadhai and the sound of cumin seeds splitting in the heat and the colour of turmeric staining his mother's fingers were memories he carried in a part of himself that had nothing to do with the ability to reproduce them in a German castle with German rations.

Cooking. The alternative would have required him to say that he was a Fellow of the Royal College of Surgeons who had never learned to cook because his family had servants and his mother considered the kitchen her domain and a Brahmin son's place was at the table, not the stove. This explanation would have confirmed everything they believed about him. So he cooked, badly, in silence, and they ate what he cooked, complained and he absorbed the complaints the way the stone floor absorbed the cold: completely, without expression, from beneath.

The mincemeat was his finest hour. A tin labelled MINCEMEAT, he had read the label, understood the English, and added the contents to the curry in the reasonable expectation that minced meat was what the tin contained. It was not. It was fruit filling: sweet, sticky, dense with raisins and candied peel, and the resulting curry was a dish no culinary tradition could classify. The British officers ate it in various stages of horror and hilarity. One man gagged. Another laughed until his eyes watered. The story circulated within the hour. It would circulate for the remainder of the war, beyond the war, into the books that would be written about the castle, and in none of these circulations would anyone record that the man who made the mincemeat curry held a diploma in tropical medicine and could identify sixteen distinct cardiac arrhythmias by auscultation alone.

He cleaned the pot. He cleaned it slowly, with hot water that was not hot enough, scrubbing the residue of fruit and spice from the metal with a cloth that was not clean, the only sound in the kitchen and the sound was his answer to all of it — to the laughter, to the name, to the tin, to the assumption that his brown skin meant his hands must know a certain skill. His hands knew other skills. But the pot was what they had given his hands to do, and so he cleaned the pot.

III

Tuesday afternoons, the escape committee met. Mazumdar knew this, the sounds changed, footsteps converging on a room at the end of the corridor, a door closing with intention rather than habit, voices lowered to the frequency of men planning something dangerous and thrilling and forbidden. He heard these sounds from whatever margin he happened to occupy.

He approached Colonel Dorian about being considered for an escape attempt. He approached him formally, as one officer to another, with the correct salutation and the correct posture, the careful English that he had learned at the Royal College of Surgeons in Edinburgh and honed across every ward and mess and consultation room since. He made his case. He was an officer. He spoke German. He spoke French. He had the right, under the Geneva Convention, to attempt escape.

Colonel Dorian looked at him as a man looks at an item that has been misplaced.

"You? Escaping from here? With your brown skin?" The colonel was right. And the colonel's rightness was the worst thing about it, the exclusion was physics, the immutable fact of his visibility in a world designed for other faces.

He stood in the courtyard after the meeting. The walls rose on every side and the men walked their circuits and the escape committee was meeting behind a door he could hear but not enter.

IV

Eduard Engles was half-Indonesian and an officer in the Dutch East Indies army and the only other person of colour in Colditz. He had a thin face, the zygomatic arches prominent beneath skin that had thinned from months of camp rations, and careful hands and the demeanour of someone who had mastered being present in a room without disturbing the room's assumptions about itself. They found each other by the simple recognition of men who are fluent in being looked through. Engles knew the practice. Mazumdar had perfected it. In the courtyard, the knowledge was mutual and required no speech.

They walked together in the courtyard. They sat together at meals. They spoke in English, which was neither man's first language, and the English they spoke had careful construction, each sentence built rather than thrown, the words chosen with the precision of men who had learned that in borrowed languages, carelessness was visible. Engles told him about Java. The heat, the green, the Dutch who governed with a politeness that was itself a form of violence. Mazumdar listened with attention that was genuine and boundaries that were invisible. The slight hesitation before a personal question, Engles' eyes searching his face for permission and finding courtesy instead. Mazumdar could see him feel the boundary. Neither of them named it. They walked their circuit day after day. The circuit was their friendship, the friendship bounded by the wire and the boundary was precisely what made it possible, what allowed the friendship to exist because without boundaries there is only the infinite and the infinite is lonely.

A French officer took him aside one afternoon. Lieutenant Boulanger — small, precise. "You know the British officers are calling you a spy. They've asked us to keep away from you."

The jaw tightened. The masseter, the quarter-millimetre. Somewhere across the courtyard a man laughed at something and the laughter continued and the courtyard continued. The word arrived from his childhood (*achut*, the one who must not be touched) and arrived in Bengali, which meant it arrived from the deepest part of him.

He thanked Boulanger. He returned to the courtyard.

V

News arrived in fragments. The prisoners had a hidden radio and the information it produced circulated through the castle with the velocity of news that cannot be verified and therefore cannot be doubted. He received the fragments late, filtered through conversations he was adjacent to rather than part of, the news arriving already shaped by other men's reactions, the shock on their faces, the lowered voices, attention that told him news had arrived before anyone told him what.

Singapore had fallen. The Japanese had taken Malaya, Burma, the Dutch East Indies. Indian soldiers, tens of thousands, were being recruited by Bose. Subhas Chandra Bose, who had escaped India in disguise, who had arrived in Berlin, who was raising an army of Indian POWs to fight the British. Men who had made the choice Mazumdar had not yet been asked to make.

Gandhi was in prison. The Quit India movement had been crushed. The Bengal countryside was in famine, the numbers were unclear, the rumours contradictory, but the word *famine* arrived with a weight that the word *war* had never carried because war was European and famine was Bengali and the famine was happening in the country he could not reach, to people he could not treat, in villages whose names he might know.

India was fighting and starving and he was in a kitchen scrubbing a pot.

Weeks passed. The courtyard did not change. He could not treat patients. The knowledge settled in him like sediment in a still glass. He was a better physician than the German camp doctor. He had diagnoses the German could not make and treatments the German did not know. Men came to the infirmary with conditions he could identify from across the room, the gait, the colour, a cough, and he sat in the courtyard, listened to the coughing and could do nothing. Officers did not work. The Geneva Convention, which protected his rights as a prisoner, also prevented him from exercising the one skill that gave his existence purpose. And so the hands that could perform an appendectomy peeled potatoes.

Red Cross parcels arrived monthly. The British officers shared them communally, chocolate, condensed milk, biscuits, tea, tinned meat. The sharing was organised by room, by mess, by the same social architecture that governed everything else. His share was what remained after the sharing was done, the biscuits halved, the condensed milk gone, the chocolate a memory of chocolate in the form of an empty wrapper that someone had left on the table. The parcels were distributed by men who knew him as Jumbo and who served him last, and serving last was not the same as serving at all.

THE IRISHMAN

Chapter 7

I

Ferguson arrived in 1942.

Mazumdar did not know, at first, that this arrival would be different from any other. Men arrived at Colditz regularly, transferred from other camps for attempted escape or general recalcitrance. Each arrival disrupted the social geometry for a day or two before the geometry absorbed the new body. Ferguson should have been absorbed.

He was not absorbed because he was Irish. Dr Ion Ferguson, an Irishman from Knockcloghrim, County Londonderry, which meant he was British as Mazumdar was British: technically, legally, with documents to prove it and a lifetime of evidence to the contrary.

Mazumdar met him in the courtyard on his first morning. Ferguson was standing by the wall, looking up at the castle's towers with the expression of arrival, recognition settling and now confronting the difference between being told and being here.

"You'll rue the day you came to this madhouse," Mazumdar said. "Most of us are cracked here."

Ferguson looked at him. The looking was different. Not the calculation, not the brown-face-wrong-face-category-search that

Mazumdar had learned to read in years of British officers' eyes. This was the look of someone told an honest thing and deciding whether the honesty is a gift or a warning. It was both. Ferguson's mouth moved. Not quite a smile. Something before a smile, the preparation for one, the face acknowledging that it has been met by a face worth meeting.

Ferguson treated Mazumdar as an equal. Ferguson's equality was unselfconscious. He did not make a point of it. He sat with Mazumdar because Mazumdar was there and Ferguson needed someone to sit with and the two men shared a quality, a stillness, a precision of speech, that made the sitting natural.

They talked. About medicine — Ferguson had been wounded and treated by field surgeons whose competence he assessed with frank curiosity, he had been cut open and would like to know how well it was done. About Ireland, the landscape, the rain, the green of Fermanagh in spring. About nothing, the silences between them comfortable in a way that silences with Engles were not, because Engles' silences contained the question Mazumdar could not answer and Ferguson's silences contained no question at all.

One evening Ferguson sat beside him on the bunk and said nothing for twenty minutes. He was simply there: large, warm, reading a book he had read before, his shoulder touching Mazumdar's shoulder. The contact was accidental or it was not. Ferguson did not move away. Mazumdar did not move away. The reading continued and the shoulder remained and the first physical warmth from another person that Mazumdar had received since he could not remember when.

Ferguson would sit with you. Not because you needed sitting with, but because sitting was what he did. Your company was as good as any, better than most, and if the sitting lasted hours or days he would not be the one to leave.

They were still on the bunk when the light changed. The afternoon sun had moved past the window and the stone had shifted colour, that particular grey of Colditz in spring when the sun appeared and then withdrew, appeared and withdrew. Ferguson turned a page. The paper made a sound. Small friction between his thumb and the edge.

"Your wound," Mazumdar said. "Where?" "Left abdomen. Below the ribs." "Clean entry?" "No. Fragmented. They did a partial debridement in the field hospital. Took out what they could see."

Mazumdar could place it, the trajectory, the bleeding, the infection likelihood. A surgeon's mathematics. "Did it heal clean?"

"Clean enough. There's adhesion. I feel it when I'm cold." Ferguson shifted his weight. Not moving away, repositioning, drawing his knee up, making room for Mazumdar's space without surrendering his own. "You would have done it differently." Not a question.

"I would have opened it wider. Checked for peritoneal penetration." Mazumdar could see the scar tissue, could trace the inflammation patterns through Ferguson's description. "The field surgeons did competent work. Which is remarkable, considering they had no time."

"But you would have had time." "Yes." Ferguson nodded. The page turned. The sound came again, thumb leaving the fibre, the paper edge sliding, the small surrender of reading. "I had an infection three months after. Fever. The camp doctor wanted to lance it. I refused."

"You were right." "I knew you'd say that." Ferguson's voice was flat. Not humorous. Simply accurate. "I waited it out. It resolved. But I knew what I was gambling with."

"And you gambled." "Yes." The silence returned. The sun retreated further. In the courtyard below, men began their late-afternoon circuit, the predictable footsteps, the gravel crunching in the same patterns it had crunched for three years. Mazumdar could hear it without looking. The rhythm was familiar as breathing.

"In Edinburgh," Mazumdar said, "I trained under a man named Chiene. He would say that a body tells you everything if you're willing to listen. He meant physically. The signs. The presentations."

"And you believe him." "I believe bodies don't lie." Ferguson turned another page. The light was nearly gone now. He was reading by the last angle of sun that came through the window, reading deliberately, not rushing. "My body told me something at Dunkirk," he said. "It told me I was going to die. And then I didn't. So now I don't listen to it."

Mazumdar heard this. The statement was complete in itself. No request. No question. Ferguson had said what he needed to say and was returning to his book.

They sat. The light left. The bell rang for tea. Neither of them moved until Ferguson set the book down and stood, carefully, not suddenly, giving Mazumdar time to withdraw his shoulder if he wanted to. He didn't want to. Ferguson's warmth had left a rectangle on his skin that would cool now, that was cooling already, and Mazumdar watched it go the way he watched everything, with precision, with registration, the body reporting what the mind refused to name.

II

The days continued. Identical. The church clock struck the hours. The men walked their circuits. The escape committee met on Tuesdays. The kitchen smelled of cabbage and the attic smelled of wool and men and in the morning the cycle began again. Appell. Breakfast. The courtyard. Lunch. The courtyard. Appell. The hours. The dark.

Stone cold. It came from the walls, the floor, the window frames. The cold of a building that had been cold for four hundred years and would be cold for four hundred more. The heating, when there was heating, made no impression on this cold, the cold was architectural, load-bearing, invisible to the men who had designed the structure because they had designed it for themselves.

He wrote Bengali poems at night. He wrote them in a small notebook beneath his mattress, small and careful, the poems were not good and the not-good did not matter, they were not for anyone. They were for the language. For the act of making Bengali words appear on paper in a castle in Saxony where no one else could read them. The pen moved. The letters curved, connected. The curves were the shapes his hand had learned in Gaya at a wooden desk that smelled of chalk and his father's study. The tongue shaped the words silently in the dark while the men around him slept. He could feel the language in his mouth, the vowels wider than English, the consonants softer, the rhythm slower, as though Bengali itself remembered a pace of life that no longer existed anywhere except in the act of writing it down.

Months passed. The months were the same month repeated. Spring arrived in the sky above the courtyard, a different blue, the smell of grass beyond the walls arriving as information rather than experience. He could smell cut grass on certain mornings when the wind came from the south, and the smell carried the world outside that was more painful than any deprivation inside, because the smell was free, arrived freely and left freely and he could not follow it. Summer. The courtyard warmer. The cobblestones held the heat of the afternoon sun and released it slowly through the evening and he could feel the warmth through the soles of his boots. He walked the margins the way a doctor walks a ward, the same route, the same pace, the body knowing the circuit.

The escape committee busier. He watched from the margins as the maps were drawn and the tunnels dug and the men moved with the suppressed electricity of purpose.

Eight months. Nine. He was the castle's Indian. The castle's doctor who could not doctor. The man who cooked the curry, cleaned the pot, walked at the margins, wrote Bengali poems that no one would read. He waited, though he did not know what he was waiting for, and the waiting had no object and no end.

Then the summons came.

III

A Tuesday in June. The Indian arrived in the courtyard during Appell, a young man in Wehrmacht field grey, standing beside the German adjutant, rigid, aware he was being looked at. The uniform was German. The face was not. The face was Indian, dark, sharp-featured, young, twenty-three or twenty-four, and the incongruity of the Indian face above the German collar produced in the courtyard a silence that was different from the silences Mazumdar had learned to read. This silence was surprise. The British officers stood in their rows and looked at the young man and did not understand what they were seeing.

Mazumdar's body recognised the pattern before his mind had named it. The badge on the young man's left breast was a leaping tiger on a tricolour ground: orange, white, green. The Indian National Congress flag. On a German uniform. In a German castle.

It meant Bose. The name had reached Colditz months earlier: fragments, rumours, the currency of information that circulates in prisons. Mazumdar had heard it first from the French, who heard everything before the British. The French said that Subhas Chandra Bose was in Berlin. That he had escaped from house arrest in Calcutta, travelled through Afghanistan and the Soviet Union, and was recruiting an Indian army to fight against the British. With the Germans.

Filing the information, he considered it in the dark, lying in his bunk, turning it as he turned everything, forming provisional understandings, discarding them, forming others. Bose in Berlin. And now the condition's emissary was standing in the courtyard at Appell.

The young man sought out Mazumdar after Appell. He walked directly across the courtyard and the British officers watched, a sharpening, a narrowing, the courtyard's attention contracting to the point where the Indian in German uniform met the Indian in British uniform.

They spoke in Hindi. The young man's Hindi was clipped, northern, recently used in the company of other Indians. Mazumdar's was slower, roughened by disuse, the vocabulary intact but the rhythm unfamiliar. The young man said he brought greetings from the Free India Centre in Berlin. He said that Netaji wished to meet him. That arrangements could be made.

He said he would consider the invitation. After a moment the young man left. The courtyard resumed its patterns. But the patterns had changed. A variable had entered the system that the system had not anticipated: Mazumdar had spoken to the visitor in a language the British could not understand, about a matter that concerned them profoundly and from which they were entirely excluded. For the first time since his arrival, Mazumdar was the one with information.

The inversion lasted hours. By evening the courtyard had recalibrated, and the recalibration was worse than the original configuration.

Whose side was he on?

THE ATTIC

Chapter 8

I

He could not sleep.

This was not unusual. Sleep at Colditz was not rest; it was the sleep of a building, partial, provisional, subject to the building's terms. The attic decided when he slept and for how long and the depth of the sleeping and the waking. Some nights the body surrendered within minutes and the surrender was complete, a dropping through the surface of consciousness into a dark that held nothing, not even the awareness of itself. Other nights the surrender did not come. Tonight the mind had the tiger badge to work on, the Hindi, the question that had followed him up the iron rungs.

On his back he lay. The ceiling was close — close enough that his breath, in winter, would have been visible against it had there been light to see it by. In summer the closeness was different: warm, intimate, the heat of the day trapped between the roof tiles and the plaster, released slowly through the night so that the attic, which was the coldest place in winter, became the warmest in summer, and the warmth was worse than the cold, the cold at least kept the mind sharp, kept it occupied with the management of temperature.

June. The longest days. The light lingered in the rectangle of the window until past ten, fading through gradations of blue that he watched, the only private act remaining to him. The sky did not know it was being watched and the watching did not change the sky.

Two years. The number had no weight when spoken. It was an administrative quantity, a figure for a form, a fact for a file. But the body knew it differently. The body knew two years as a thickness in the joints when he swung his legs off the bunk each morning. As a looseness in the waistband of his trousers that had not been loose when he arrived. As a slowness in the right shoulder, the deltoid, the supraspinatus, that had appeared without injury or exertion, the body dismantling itself from disuse as a house dismantles from neglect, one small failure at a time, each insignificant, the total devastating.

The men below him slept. The sleeping was a sound, a composition, a layering of breathing and shifting and the small involuntary vocalisations of men whose bodies spoke only when the men were not conscious to prevent them. Someone muttered. The muttering was in English but the English was disassembled, the syntax of a man dreaming in a language he no longer fully controlled. Someone else coughed, the dry, brief cough of a man coughing in his sleep, the body clearing its passages while the mind was elsewhere. The iron bunks creaked, the metal adjusting to the weight of the bodies and the bodies adjusting to the metal.

Awake, and they were asleep. The sleeping men were absent, their bodies present, warm, heavy, but the men themselves had gone somewhere he could not follow. They had left the castle. They had left the attic. They had left the war. They were in England, in New Zealand, in the rooms of their childhoods, and the rooms received them without question, and the men moved through these rooms with the freedom of sleepers, which is the only freedom that cannot be confiscated.

The wool of the blanket was rough against his neck. It smelled of other men's sleep, a smell he had learned to identify by its components, damp wool, unwashed hair, the sourness of exhalation accumulated over hours, and could not learn to ignore. The smell was the attic. He breathed it in, the only thing he shared with the men around him.

He could not join them. He had tried the countermeasures, counting, anatomical sequences, the brachial plexus, the twelve cranial nerves, Bengali poetry committed to memory in a previous life, the breathing exercises his mother had taught him as a child, exercises she said came from the sadhus at Bodh Gaya. The exercises calmed the body. The mind continued.

II

It followed him to the attic. The question climbed the iron rungs behind him and lay beside him on the mattress and breathed beside him in the dark, a presence as real as the men in the bunks below, as constant as the church clock that struck the hours with the indifference of a mechanism that did not know what it was counting.

He was on the King's side. He had said so at Kassel. He had said so at Marienberg. He had said so at every intermediate camp where a German officer or an Indian collaborator had put the question to him. The answer had been the same each time, a fact, not an argument, something that had happened, something that could not be undone by subsequent events any more than a surgical incision could be undone by the patient's subsequent dissatisfaction with the scar.

Like an incision, the oath was. The registrar had once told him, the pause before the incision is where the doctor becomes a doctor. Not the cut. The pause. The moment when the hand is steady on the body and the mind is empty. The oath was that pause stretched into seven years, the hand steady, the mind empty.

In the dark, when the examination began, the oath was what he returned to. Not the words, he did not need to recall the words, the words were in him as the anatomy was in him, memorised so thoroughly that the memorisation had become structure rather than content, knowledge the body held without the mind's participation.

What he returned to was the room. The recruiting office. September 1939.

It was in London. A building he had walked past hundreds of times without entering, stone façade, brass letters, the institutional solidity of a building that exists to process human decisions into administrative facts. He had entered it on a Tuesday. He remembered the day, the surgery closed, his Tuesday afternoon off, and he had spent the morning seeing patients and the afternoon walking from his rooms in Bayswater to the recruiting office in a state of mind that he could not, lying in the attic nearly three years later, accurately reconstruct. It had not been excitement. It had not been patriotism as the English understood patriotism, the flag, the King, the sentimentality that substituted for political analysis. Something closer to a certainty that had finally arrived.

The war had been declared three weeks earlier. The patients in his surgery, English patients, who came to him, he was a good doctor, and they stayed despite his face or perhaps, some of them, because of it, had been talking about it. The men were restless. The women were frightened. The newspapers carried the news with the barely suppressed excitement of an industry that had been waiting for this event for years. And Mazumdar had listened and read and understood that the question was when to join, not whether. Because the alternative: sitting in his surgery while other men fought, treating the coughs and sprains and varicose veins of a civilian population while the world determined the century's shape, was not available to a man who had spent his life proving that he belonged to the institution that was now asking its members to fight.

Wooden, polished — the floor of the recruiting office had a smell that he could recall with a precision that astonished him, lying in the attic, a chemical sweetness, institutional, the smell of a building that was cleaned by people who did not work in it for people who did. There was a desk. Behind the desk was a sergeant: young, moustached, efficient with the brisk competence of men who process forms. The form was long. It asked questions that assumed certain answers: name, rank, nationality. He wrote INDIAN under nationality. The sergeant looked at the word and then at Mazumdar and then at the word again, the calculation of a man determining whether the system he served had anticipated this arrival.

It had not. But the system adjusted, as systems do, and the form was completed and the oath was administered. He stood. He raised his right hand. On the wall behind the sergeant was a photograph of King George VI, the thin face, the naval uniform, someone who had not expected to be King and carried the surprise in his jaw. Mazumdar faced the photograph and spoke the words, the words were in English and the English was his best English, the language by which he had built his life in this country that was now asking him to die for it.

I swear by Almighty God that I will be faithful and bear true allegiance to His Majesty King George the Sixth, his heirs and successors, and that I will, as in duty bound, honestly and faithfully defend His Majesty, his heirs and successors, in person, crown and dignity against all enemies.

The words filled the room. He lowered his hand. The sergeant made a note. The floor polish was still sweet and the photograph was still on the wall, King George's jaw was still carrying its surprise and Mazumdar was, from that moment, a soldier of the Crown, an officer of the Royal Army Medical Corps, a man who had given his word.

The blanket had slipped. His left shoulder was bare to the attic air, the cold settling on the deltoid, and he pulled the wool back without shifting his gaze from the ceiling.

Not the King, not the flag, not the Empire, the word. The word was the thing. The oath was his word and his word was him and the giving of it was irreversible, a word, once given, exists outside the giver the way a child, once born, exists outside the mother. He could not take it back. He could not qualify it. The oath did not permit reservations.

His left knee had locked. He shifted, the bunk frame pressing a new pattern into his hip.

A beam above him settled, the timber contracting in the cooling night. The sound was brief, absorbed by the stone.

It was total. And his giving of it was total. And the totality was what he carried now, in the attic, in the dark, years after the oath had failed to protect him from anything the oath was supposed to protect him from.

III

Pressure. The ceiling pressed down on him with the pressure of a thought that has no exit, a thought that arrives and remains and cannot be expelled.

Was it worth it. The question did not arrive as a question. It arrived as a sensation, a loosening, a shift in the structure that held the oath in place inside him, as a hairline fracture in a load-bearing wall is felt first as a change in the building's acoustics before it is visible as a crack. He felt the shift and recognised it and filed it as he filed everything: observed, noted, deferred. The masseter tightened. The jaw held.

Was it worth it. The oath that made him British and the Britishness that did not recognise the oath. The King's commission and the kitchen, the curry and the chair near the draught and the bunk at the back of the attic and the name, Jumbo, always Jumbo — the name that was not a name but a verdict. The oath had made him a soldier and the soldiers did not include him in their escape plans. The oath had made him an officer and the officers sent him to cook. The oath had made him a gentleman and the gentlemen excluded him from their conversations, their committees and their distribution of Red Cross parcels and their plans for the tunnel that was, even now, being dug beneath the chapel while he lay in the attic above it, the furthest point from the freedom being excavated below.

And now Bose. The name in the courtyard. The badge on the uniform. The tiger leaping on the tricolour. The invitation.

Bose had not taken the oath. Bose had taken a different oath, to India, to freedom, to a logic that required allies and did not examine the allies too closely. Bose had looked at the system and seen what

Mazumdar had not allowed himself to see. Not the contract. The hallucination. The Britishness was the hallucination. The oath was the mechanism by which the hallucination sustained itself, the ritual repetition that made the fiction feel like fact.

He could hear Bose's argument without having heard it. The curry did not change whether it was cooked by a loyal officer or a colonised subject. The exclusion did not change. The bunk did not change. Only the meaning changed. And the meaning changed the man.

Somewhere below, a man coughed. The cough was dry, brief, the single contraction of a diaphragm clearing fluid from a bronchus. The attic absorbed it.

Was it worth it. Answering was not possible. The question was not asking to be answered. It was asking to be held — held the way a weight is held when the arms are tired and when the distance to ground is not visible and when the holding stretches into a kind of endlessness, the decision, once made, could not be unmade, and the unmaking would mean that the oath, the oath that was him, that he had made himself from, was a fracture, and the fracture, once seen, could not be unseen.

His hip ached. The left hip, the bunk's iron frame pressing through the mattress into the bone, a dull compression he shifted away from and shifted back to.

Three in the morning. The church clock's sound entered the attic through wall and window. The sound was old — older than the war, older than the castle's current function, the sound of a mechanism that had been counting hours since before the men in this attic were born and would continue counting after they were gone. Three in the morning. The hour at which the body's temperature is lowest, the hour at which the most people die.

He turned onto his side. The bunk creaked. Someone below shifted in response, the unconscious sympathy of a sleeping body registering a disturbance in its environment.

The window held a darkness that was not quite dark, the summer sky retaining light even at three in the morning, a greyness, a memory of the day that had passed and a premonition of the day that would come.

Tomorrow the courtyard. Tomorrow the kitchen. Tomorrow the same men in the same patterns. Tomorrow the question, present in the eyes of the British officers who had watched the Indian emissary cross the courtyard to speak to the Indian prisoner in a language they could not understand.

Tomorrow. But not tonight. Tonight the question existed only in the attic, between the ceiling and the mattress. The body was cold and tired and subject to the building's terms. The mind was in the recruiting office in London in September 1939, standing before a photograph of a King, giving a word that could not be taken back.

The church clock counted. The attic breathed around him. He lay still, and the stillness preceded a decision not yet made, held breath.

Through the window he watched. The grey lightened by fractions. The pigeons stirred in the eaves above him, the first sound of morning, low and persistent. Then the flutter of wings against tile as one of them left the roof, crossed the window's frame of sky and was gone.

He would go to Berlin. The decision was forming in the part of him that made decisions — beneath the oath, beneath the question, beneath the months of courtyard and kitchen and attic, the part that was neither British nor Indian but simply alive, simply a body in a bunk in a castle in Saxony that had been given an invitation and would accept it.

For now there was the ceiling and the breathing and the clock and the window's slow greying and the oath and the stone and the dark pressing down on him with the same weight, at the same distance, and neither the oath nor the stone would move first.

THE ACCUSATION

Chapter 9

I

Cold tiles, iron pipes, the smell of calcium. Six in the morning. The light came from a high window: grey, early, the light of a building that did not care whether the men inside it could see.

Cleaning his teeth. The toothbrush was worn, the bristles splayed, the handle cracked, and the motion of the brushing was automatic, the arm performing its function while the mind performed a different function, which was the preparation for a thing he could not anticipate.

The voice came from behind him. "That bloody Mazumdar is a spy. He's going to Berlin." English, the voice, loud enough to be heard by every man in the washroom and calibrated to sound as though it were not intended to be heard by the man it concerned. The British art of saying something directly by saying it indirectly. The insult delivered as observation. Mazumdar knew the technique. He had been its subject since he arrived. He turned.

Captain Harry Ellingham stood at the far end of the washroom. Six feet two. Guardsman. One of the first British officers sent to Colditz, an officer who had been in the castle long enough to believe the castle belonged to him. Ellingham's face was sharp, confident, amused. The amusement was the worst part, he had said what he thought and did not expect consequences, had never experienced consequences from men who look like Mazumdar.

Quiet, the washroom. Five or six officers, shaving, washing, had stopped. The razors were still. The taps dripped.

Mazumdar was aware of the space between them. Twelve feet. The tiles. His toothbrush in his right hand, the foam on his chin, the tap running behind him. He was aware of the height difference, Ellingham six-two, himself five-seven, and the awareness was mathematical, the body calculating angles as it had once calculated angles in surgical theatre.

"Harry." His voice was level. "Did I hear you say I am a spy?"

Ellingham looked down at him. The looking-down was literal and the literalness was the insult's architecture, a tall man looking at a short man, a white man looking at a brown man.

"I give you five minutes to withdraw this accusation." The words arrived from the same place the oath had arrived, from the part of him that made decisions without consulting the rest. The five minutes was a formality. Ellingham would not withdraw. But the formality mattered. The formality was the code, his father's code, the code of honour and fidelity that did not bend in crisis, that classified a man who broke his word with the quadrupeds. He was offering Ellingham the courtesy of time. Five minutes. The length of a consultation. Ellingham laughed.

Five minutes. They passed in the washroom's cold light, in the dripping tap and the breathing of men who were watching, the silence of a building that had contained every accumulated humiliation of his captivity and was about to hear what that accumulation sounds like when it reaches the surface.

His blood tingled. The sensation started in his feet, a heat, a rising, a current that moved upward through his calves and thighs, chest and arms. It arrived in his right fist as a thing he recognised.

No longer holding a toothbrush, the right hand released it. The toothbrush fell to the floor. The hand was a fist.

The fist travelled. Three feet. The angle compensating for the height. It connected with Ellingham's jaw, not the crack of boxing films but a wet, dense, percussive thing, bone meeting bone through skin. The shock travelled up his arm into his shoulder.

Ellingham went down. He fell. Slowly. Knees first, then hips, then shoulders, the height that had been the insult's architecture now its weakness, the body's secret that the mind had always known, the taller the man, the further the distance to recover. The tiles received him with the flat indifference of a surface designed for standing, not for falling.

Mazumdar was on his chest. He did not remember the transition from standing to kneeling. His knees were on the cold tiles and his hands were on Ellingham and the hands were not a surgeon's hands, they were hands that had cooked curry and scrubbed pots and peeled potatoes and been called Jumbo and excluded from escape plans and served last and slept in the coldest bunk and waited, waited, waited month after month in a castle that treated him as furniture, and the hands were speaking.

"I'll kill you." The voice was his. He did not recognise it. "You don't know what I've gone through."

Arms pulled him off. Three men. Four. They gripped his shoulders, his elbows. They pulled him backward across the tiles and the scraping of his knees on the cold surface was the sound of the washroom reasserting its function.

On his feet. The men released him. His breathing was rough, rapid, the cardiovascular system responding to a sudden demand with the efficiency of a system that had not forgotten how.

Ellingham was on the floor. Sitting. His jaw already swelling, the soft tissue responding to trauma with the predictable cascade Mazumdar could have described, clinically, with his eyes closed. Blood at the corner of Ellingham's mouth. Not much. Enough.

The washroom was silent. The watching was different now, recalibration, the shift that follows a thing that cannot be taken back. The same room but different. The understanding of the walls revised.

He wiped the foam from his chin with the back of his hand.

II

Stanhope had replaced Dorian as Senior British Officer while Mazumdar was in Berlin.

Colonel Stanhope's office was small and cold and the colonel behind the desk was a man who administered a system that administered men. Mazumdar stood before him.

"You struck a senior officer." "Yes, sir." "Captain Ellingham is a Guardsman. You are aware —"

"He called me a spy, sir." The sentence stopped Stanhope. Not because the accusation was surprising, the castle's opinion of Mazumdar was known. The sentence delivered without deference, without the careful English Mazumdar had perfected since arriving at the castle.

"I told him the reason," Mazumdar said. "He didn't believe me."

Stanhope looked at him. The looking was someone encountering a case the system did not anticipate, a brown officer who strikes a white officer and is both wrong and right, and the system had no mechanism for processing a man who was both.

"You are travelling to Berlin this morning." "Yes, sir." "I expect a full report on your return." *On your return,* the closest Stanhope would come to acknowledging that Mazumdar might return. The conditional was built into the phrasing, the future tense that did not believe in the future it described. Mazumdar heard it. He heard everything.

"Yes, sir." Out of the office. The corridor was long and cold and his footsteps were the only sound, a man walking toward a door that opened onto a courtyard that opened onto a gate that opened onto a road that led to Berlin.

III

They gave him clothes. Not his own: better, pressed, the uniform cleaned and repaired. The Germans wanted him presentable. The presentation was a message, the man arriving in Berlin should not look like someone who had been scrubbing pots. He should look like a King's Commissioned Officer, a King's Commissioned Officer was what Bose wanted.

He dressed. The uniform fit differently: looser in the shoulders, the body having changed its proportions in captivity. Someone had polished his buttons. The polishing was a small violence, the Germans preparing him as one prepares a gift.

Engles found him at the bunk. "Berlin." He said it without inflection. A fact, not a question.

"Berlin." Engles sat on the edge of the lower bunk. He was quiet for a time. Through the window, the courtyard was already active, men walking their circuits, the morning continuing as though a washroom floor had not been bloodied twenty minutes earlier.

"You'll come back," Engles said. It was not a prediction. It was an instruction, and the instruction surprised him, because Engles had never before spoken with this directness, had maintained always a careful distance, their friendship bounded by limits both men understood. The washroom had shifted them. Mazumdar looked at him, at the thin face, the careful hands, and understood that Engles was the only person in the castle who believed this, and that the believing was conviction, and that the conviction was a thing he would carry to Berlin close to the body, invisible, essential.

"I'll come back." The guard escort waited in the courtyard. Two soldiers, correct, indifferent. A car beyond the gate.

He stood in the courtyard one last time. The rectangle. The cobblestones he had walked for months, each crack, each uneven surface, the margins he had made his own. The walls rising on three sides. The chapel. The sky above, pale blue, Saxon, June.

Men watched from the windows. He could feel them, faces at the glass, the watching that had defined his existence here turned now to a different purpose. They were watching him leave. Some believed he was going to betray them. Some believed he already had. One, perhaps only one, perhaps Engles at the window of the bunk he had just left, believed he would come back.

We never expected to see him again. He did not hear this. He would hear it years later, the sentence arriving as information about a moment he had lived through without knowing what the moment looked like from above. At the time there were only the cobblestones and the gate and the guard and the morning air that smelled of something other than stone, something green, distant, free, and the smell was so unfamiliar that he stopped at the gate and breathed it in, and the breath was the first free breath he had taken in two years and the freedom of it was a physical shock, a widening in the chest, as if the lungs had been held at partial capacity by the building itself and were now remembering their full size.

He got into the car. The gate closed behind him. The castle rose above — grey, massive — and then diminished as the road descended, getting smaller in the rear window, smaller, until it was the size of a fist, and then gone.

THE TRAIN

Chapter 10

I

Green. Ordinary. The countryside was farms, trees, a woman hanging laundry — and the ordinariness was a kind of violence because it proved that the world had continued without him, had continued being ordinary while he was inside the stone, and the continuation did not require his presence or his absence or his oath or his name or anything about him at all.

The guard in the front seat did not speak. The driver did not speak. The car smelled of leather and petrol and the driver's tobacco. Mazumdar sat in the back with his hands on his knees and the countryside passing, a problem, because the eyes had lost the habit of distance. Two years of walls, the courtyard's twenty-seven metres, the attic ceiling an arm's length above, the kitchen's low stone arch. The eyes had learned to stop at surfaces. Now the surfaces had been removed and the eyes went out across the fields and found no wall.

A river. He saw it from the road, a flat brown surface running through pasture, the sun catching it in places, a bridge ahead. The car crossed the bridge and the river was beneath them for three seconds, then behind them and the seeing of it opened a door, not a thought but a sensation, a door in the chest that had been there all along waiting to be opened, the body registering water as the body registers the voice of someone it has not heard in years.

The Phalgu. He had swum in it as a boy. His father standing on the ghat, watching. The water warm and shallow, his feet finding the sandy bottom and the sand shifting beneath him with each step, the ground not quite solid, the river's underground current detectable through the soles, a pressure, a pull, a movement beneath the stillness. The Phalgu at Gaya. The river that ran through the town where his father practised and his mother cooked, the mango tree grew in the courtyard and the temple bells sounded at dawn.

The word arrived from the place where Bengali lived, beneath the English, beneath the medical vocabulary, beneath the two years of institutional language that had become his primary tongue. *Phalgu.* The river that went underground each summer. The bed dried, the sand stretched white, people walked across it as if it were a road. But the water still moved. The priests at Vishnupad dug shallow wells in the riverbed and the water rose, the same river, flowing in the dark.

Around a corner, the river was gone. His knuckles ached. The right hand, the striking hand. He flexed the fingers and the flexing produced a small bright pain in the metacarpophalangeal joints, Ellingham's jaw, the tiles, the voice he had not recognised as his own.

The aching was not regret.

II

First class. He sat in the compartment and the seat was upholstered and the upholstery gave beneath his weight, a sensation he had forgotten, the sensation of a surface designed to receive a human body gently. The train moved. The landscape slid past: Saxon villages, fields, the country he was at war with and captive in and travelling through in first-class comfort toward the man who wanted to free him from the men he had sworn to serve.

Opposite him, the guard. A young soldier, nineteen or twenty, with the patient blankness of a man performing a duty he did not understand. The guard's rifle was propped between his knees. His boots were polished. He looked out the window at the countryside that was his.

Mazumdar looked at his own hands. They were on the armrests, the left relaxed, the right swollen at the knuckles, the skin across the metacarpals tight and discoloured. A doctor's hands. A cook's hands. A prisoner's hands.

Warmth. A heating element beneath the seat, he could feel it through his trousers, a low steady warmth that rose into his thighs and lower back. The body did not trust it. At Colditz, warmth was temporary, a cup of something hot held between the palms, the brief hour when the afternoon sun reached the courtyard's western wall. This warmth was continuous. It came from the train, and the train was German, and the Germans were heating him because the comfortable man is the persuadable man.

He understood this.

Saxon hills gave way to flatter ground, industrial outskirts, a factory with a tall chimney trailing smoke, a rail yard where freight cars sat in rows. The train did not stop.

A woman in the corridor. He saw her through the glass partition, middle-aged, well-dressed, carrying a leather bag. She glanced into the compartment. Her eyes found Mazumdar and moved past, returned and stayed. Two seconds, three. The brown face, the British uniform, the German guard. She walked on.

Eyes closed. Behind them the landscape continued, he could feel the train's movement, the slight sway, the rhythm of the rails, each beat a metre closer to the man who would ask him to betray everything the last two years had cost him.

III

Afternoon. The guard fell asleep, the rifle between his knees, the chin dropping. Mazumdar watched him sleep. The boy's face in sleep was soft, unfinished. A farmer's son, probably.

You'll come back. Engles's instruction, riding with him. By morning he would shake Bose's hand. The same hand. The contradiction sat beside him like a second passenger and neither of them spoke. Berlin by evening.

Outskirts first, apartment blocks, grey, uniform. Then the train slowed. The buildings thickened, the tracks multiplied beneath them. The sound changed, the rhythm of open country becoming the stutter of points and junctions, the train threading itself into the city's system.

The station. He stepped onto the platform. The guard was beside him: awake now, correct, the rifle back on his shoulder.

The air was different from Saxon air: warmer, denser, carrying the smells of a city at war: diesel, coal, something chemical, and beneath these the compressed human smell of a station where thousands pass through daily.

Bengali. He heard it. Two men on the platform, Indian, civilian clothes, speaking Bengali. The words reached him across thirty feet of station noise, physical, a hand on the arm, a grip. He had not heard Bengali spoken by someone other than himself in two years. The vowels were rounder than his, Calcutta Bengali, the same language, and hearing it unlocked what the river had opened on the road that morning. The Phalgu. The water beneath the sand. The language beneath the languages. Moving in the dark, giving no sign, surfacing now in a station in Berlin because two strangers were speaking the words his mother spoke.

The guard steered him toward the exit. A car was waiting. Berlin. The city was larger than he had imagined and darker, the blackout already beginning, the buildings losing their edges in the dusk. The car moved through streets he did not know toward a man he had admired since he was fourteen years old.

His right hand ached.

THE ROOM

Chapter 11

I

The room was large and the desk was large and the man who rose from behind it was not.

This was the first thing Mazumdar registered. A balding, bespectacled figure wearing a civilian suit, grey, well-cut, unremarkable, who stood and extended his hand and was, in the act of standing, revealed to be of ordinary height. Five feet seven. Perhaps eight. The posture compensated. The shoulders were back and the chin was level and the eyes behind the spectacles held an attention Mazumdar recognised from surgical theatre, eyes that had already assessed you before you finished entering the room.

"Doctor Mazumdar." The voice was soft. Authoritative in the way that soft voices are authoritative when they belong to men who do not need to raise them. Bengali cadence beneath the English, the vowels rounder, the consonants less percussive. Mazumdar took the hand. It was dry and firm and smaller than his own.

He did not yet know that this hand had, three days earlier, shaken the Führer's.

An admirer since age fourteen. He had read the speeches, followed the escape from India, the house arrest in Calcutta, the Abwehr's assistance, the disguise as a Pathan insurance agent named Muhammad Ziauddin, a tall Bengali with round spectacles and the bearing of a revolutionary posing as a salesman from the frontier, spirited through Peshawar into Afghanistan and then through the Soviet Union under the alias Count Orlando Mazzotta, arriving in Berlin in April 1941 with nothing but the cause and the will to pursue it. The journey was the man: audacious, theatrical, requiring a capacity for self-reinvention that was itself a kind of genius. He had imagined this man as large. Men who are larger than life are, in the imagination, large. The reality was a man of ordinary dimensions in a grey suit in a room that smelled of furniture polish and, beneath the furniture polish, cigarette smoke and the staleness of a building that has been recently renovated and not yet fully aired.

He could not speak. His mouth was dry and his hands were at his sides and this was happening, standing in front of Subhas Chandra Bose with nothing in his mouth.

Bose smiled. It was a smile that had been used before and knew its effect.

"Join my Legion," Bose said. The voice was still soft. "Come and fight for the freedom of India. Our Motherland."

Mazumdar said nothing. The nothing was not refusal. It was the absence of the mechanism that produces speech.

Bose watched him. Then, "I am an example of someone who has always struggled for my country's freedom. Join me."

Mazumdar heard himself say, "I have given my word of honour and cannot go back on this."

The words arrived from somewhere he had not consciously consulted. They were in English. They sounded, in this room, in front of this man, like words from a phrasebook, correct and hollow and belonging to a language that was not the language of the moment.

Bose's smile did not change. "Let us have some lunch."

II

The meal was served in Bose's private quarters, a smaller room, warmer, with a table set for two and a window that let in the smell of cut grass from the Tiergarten below. The waiter wore white gloves. Mazumdar watched the gloves move across the tablecloth as the dishes were laid out. He had not seen white gloves on brown hands performing a gesture of service that was not servitude in two years.

The food. He could not determine, later, whether the food was Bengali or merely Indian or simply food: real food, hot food, food that had been prepared with the intention of being eaten by a person rather than the intention of keeping a body functional. There was rice. There was dal. There was something with fish, mustard, he thought, the sharp yellow heat of it arriving at the back of his throat before the taste reached his tongue, and the taste, when it arrived, flooded his mouth. His salivary glands responded before he could. Home arriving through the palate before the mind had decided anything about homes.

Bose ate slowly. He talked while he ate — about Gaya, about Bihar, about Mazumdar's family. Narrow clavicles, the wrists fine beneath the cuffs, the build of rhetoric and nervous energy rather than physical labour. He knew things. Not intelligence-briefing things, not the dossier knowledge of an operative, but the knowledge of a Bengali who understood that a man from Gaya would have a particular relationship to the river, to the temple, to the specific quality of summer heat that sits on the plains south of Patna like a hand.

They spoke Bengali. He had not spoken Bengali, sustained, flowing, conversational Bengali, since India. The language moved between them: shared, easy, each sentence opening the next, subordinate phrase leading to subordinate phrase, the verb arriving late, the meaning accumulating in the journey rather than the destination. Like the food. But unlike the food, the language arrived from the place his body had forgotten.

Bose asked about his medical training. Mazumdar told him, the Royal College, the FRCS, the surgical rotations. He found himself talking with a fluency that surprised him. The listener was unfamiliar. Bose listened the way Mazumdar's father had listened, with his whole body inclined forward, the spectacles catching the light, the attention absorptive, as if what was being said mattered because of this person, this room.

The Bengali, the warmth, the white gloves, the fish with mustard — all arrived together in different registers, composing the same argument.

He knew what this was. The knowing did not diminish the effect, in the same way that knowing how morphine works does not diminish the relief.

The coffee came. Real coffee — coffee that tasted of coffee, dark and bitter and slightly sweet, served in a white cup on a white saucer by the gloved hands, and the taste of it sat on his tongue and would not leave and three hours later, lying in clean sheets, it would still be there, the last physical evidence of a room he had already left.

Bose pushed his cup aside. The tablecloth between them was spotted with dal, coffee, the faint yellow stain of turmeric. Neither of them had noticed the stains accumulating and the stains were evidence of time passing, of food shared, of two men eating together who had forgotten to be careful. The meal was over. The warmth remained but the air in the room had thinned, as air thins before a change in weather.

"Let me tell you," Bose said, "what I have been doing."

III

Bose stood. He paced, three steps to the window, turn, three steps back, thinking with his body, and Mazumdar remained seated, watched him move and the dynamic between them shifted with the vertical. Bose above, moving, the energy of argument in his legs and shoulders. Mazumdar below, still, the energy of reception in his silence.

Bose talked about India. Three hundred and fifty million people governed by one hundred thousand British administrators. An army of two and a half million Indian soldiers fighting for a king who would not grant them the franchise. A famine building in Bengal while the grain was shipped to feed the war. He talked about the Congress, about Gandhi, about the Quit India movement.

"I tried their way," Bose said. "I was president of the Congress. Twice. Elected by the membership. And Gandhi's faction pushed me out because my methods were too direct." He stopped at the window. "I was elected by the people and removed by the party. That is British democracy as practised by Indians. We have learned their system so well we use it against each other."

He turned from the window. "I sat the Indian Civil Service examination in London. Did you know that? Fourth in all of England. Fourth. And do you know what happened when I arrived at my posting? My district commissioner, someone who had finished below me in the same examination, addressed me by my surname without the prefix. Not Mr Bose. Not even Bose. Just the surname, the way you call a servant. I had outperformed him on his own examination in his own language and he could not bring himself to call me Mister."

He sat down. His breathing was audible — slightly elevated, the respiratory rate elevated, cardiovascular capacity not matching rhetorical output. "That was nineteen twenty-one. I resigned from the Civil Service the same year. You know what your Colditz officers are, Doctor? They are that district commissioner. Repeated across three hundred years and a hundred thousand postings. The individual is not the problem. The system is the problem. And you have sworn your oath to the system."

"I know the system," Mazumdar said. "I trained inside it. I operated inside it. The scalpel I held did not care who was holding it. The training that taught me to use it did not check the colour of my hands."

"And the training that taught you to use it, who designed it? Whose anatomy textbooks? Whose examination boards? Whose portrait on the wall of the Royal College?"

Mazumdar did not answer. "That is a distinction the system encourages you to make," Bose said. "Between the knowledge and the institution that owns the knowledge. The scalpel is neutral. The hand that gives you the scalpel is not."

He talked about the Tiger Legion. A thousand Indian soldiers had joined, men captured in North Africa, in Libya, men who had fought for Britain and been abandoned by Britain and chose, in their captivity, to fight for India instead. They wore the tiger badge against the Indian tricolour. They had purpose, a reason to be alive that did not depend on the goodwill of the men who had captured them.

"These men were sepoys," Bose said. "Farmers' sons. Villagers. They did not have your education. They did not have your commission. And they found the courage to change sides. Not for Germany. For India."

He let the sentence sit. Talking about the German alliance with candour that disarmed the obvious objection, he continued. "I am not in full agreement with the Nazi philosophy," he said. "And I candidly told them so." He paused. The spectacles caught the late afternoon light from the window. "But I hope to gain India's independence through Nazi help."

He described his meeting with Hitler, the monologue, rambling, fixated on the collapse of the British Empire, uninterested in India as anything other than a lever. "He sees India as a geographical expression," Bose said. "I see it as a nation. We are using each other, the Führer and I. The question is who will use whom more effectively." Mazumdar listened.

"You have recruited hundreds," he said. "From the camps. Sepoys. Havildars. VCOs. Men who enlisted for a wage and were taken prisoner and saw no reason to remain loyal to a king they had never seen."

Bose stopped pacing. "Are you suggesting their commitment is less than yours?"

"I am suggesting their oath was different from mine." "And your oath is superior?" "My oath is mine." "Then tell me about your oath, Doctor." Bose sat down. He sat across the table and the pacing stopped and what replaced it was a stillness more forceful than the movement.

"Tell me about the day you swore it. In Poona, yes? The recruiting office. You raised your hand. You said the words. You became a British officer. And what did the British give you in return?"

Mazumdar said nothing. The correction did not matter. He let it pass.

"I will tell you what they gave you. They gave you a commission that your fellow officers do not respect. They gave you a rank that does not protect you from being called 'the Indian.' They gave you a castle where you eat alone."

"That is not the oath's fault." "No. It is the oath's cost. And you are paying it. And the men who hold the oath, the British officers, the War Office, the King, they are not paying it. You are paying the full price of a contract in which only one party keeps its word."

A clock somewhere in the building struck five. The sound was thin and distant and neither of them acknowledged it.

"Not one King's Commissioned Officer from the British Army has joined," Bose said. "Not one. You could be the first."

"I know." "Do you know what that would mean? A man of your standing, your training, your commission, standing beside me. It would say to every Indian soldier in every camp in Europe, the British do not deserve your loyalty."

"I know what it would mean." "Then why?" Mazumdar looked at his hands. They were on the table, on either side of the empty coffee cup, and they were steady.

"Because I swore the oath," he said. "And the oath does not contain a clause for when the institution proves unworthy of it."

Bose leaned forward. “You have described a symptom and called it a principle.”

The afternoon became evening. Bose loosened his tie. The room smelled of cigarette smoke now, he had been smoking through the argument and the smoke had layered itself over the furniture polish and the remnants of the food until the air itself tasted different, thicker.

“The war will end,” Bose said. “Singapore has fallen. Malaya. Burma. When it ends, will India be free? Only if Indians have fought for it. Not for the British. For India.”

Mazumdar pushed back. “The Nazis,” he said. “Your allies. They consider us subhuman. The racial laws —”

“I know the racial laws.” “Then you know what happens to your Legion if Germany wins. You will have traded one set of masters for another. Masters who have written into law what the British only practise by convention.”

“Germany will not win.” “Then what happens to the thousand men wearing the tiger badge when Germany loses? They will be tried as traitors by the British and abandoned by the Germans. You know this.”

The room went quiet. Bose did not answer immediately. He stood and walked to the window, hands clasped behind his back. Mazumdar watched the hands, the fingers interlaced, the knuckles white, and he recognised the posture.

“Every revolution requires men who are willing to lose,” Bose said, to the window.

“Every doctor has heard that from a patient who has chosen a treatment that will kill him.”

Bose turned. The light was behind him and his face was in shadow. “You are diagnosing me, Doctor.”

“I am observing.” “And what is your observation?” “That you are brilliant. That you are sincere. That you love India as much as any man alive. And that the instrument you have chosen to free India will destroy the men who hold it before it achieves anything. The Legion is a propaganda tool for the Germans. You know this. The men in it, the farmers' sons, the villagers, they believe they are fighting for India. They are fighting for a photograph in a German newspaper."

Bose sat down. He reached for the cigarette case and took out a cigarette and lit it. The match flared and in the flare Mazumdar saw his face, the jaw set, the eyes narrowed behind the spectacles, the nostrils drawing the smoke in with the controlled breath of a man steadying himself. The cigarette burned. Bose did not speak. He smoked and the smoke climbed toward the ceiling and the room waited.

"You may be right," he said, finally. His voice was very quiet. "You may be right about all of it. And it does not change anything. Because the alternative, your alternative, Doctor, is to sit in a castle and wait for the men who despise you to win a war and then hope that they reward your patience with the freedom they have denied you for three hundred years. That is not a strategy. That is a prayer."

A bird was singing somewhere in the Tiergarten. Mazumdar could hear it through the window, a high, clear sound, absurd in its ordinariness. Bose heard it too. He turned toward the window. The bird sang. The room held the sound as it had held everything, the argument, the food, the Bengali, the coffee, without choosing sides.

Neither of them spoke. The bird stopped. The Tiergarten was quiet.

"I am opposed to the British rule in India," Mazumdar said. "I have seen the results. But I have sworn an oath of allegiance to Britain."

"And the oath is not contingent on Britain's behaviour?" Bose said.

"No."

"Then the oath is a cage. And you are choosing to remain in it."

"The oath is mine. I chose it. I cannot unchoose it because the choosing has become inconvenient."

"Inconvenient." Bose's voice was very quiet. "Is that what you call Colditz? The racism? The men who won't eat with you? Inconvenient?"

IV

The evening settled into a register that was not argument and was not peace. The waiter had come and gone a final time, a tray of biscuits that neither of them touched, a fresh pot of tea that cooled beside them. The sounds of the building receded. Staff leaving. Doors closing along the corridor. The Free India Centre becoming, by degrees, a place where two men sat in the remnant light from a single lamp.

Bose told him about the escape from India. Not the version that had appeared in the newspapers, the daring flight, the Pathan disguise, but the version that included the things that did not appear. The cold in Afghanistan. The Soviet handlers who regarded him with suspicion. The months in Berlin when no one returned his calls and he sat in a hotel room eating bad German food and wondering whether he had traded everything for nothing. The first meeting with Hitler, who talked for two hours and listened for none and left him with the understanding that India, to the Führer, was a romantic abstraction, a lever against Britain, not a nation.

"I know what I am doing," Bose said. "I know who these people are. I know what they think of us." He removed his spectacles and cleaned them on his tie and without the spectacles his face was different — younger, more exposed, the eyes blinking in the lamp light. "Do you think I sleep well, Doctor?"

Mazumdar did not answer. The removal of the spectacles was either a calculated vulnerability or a genuine one and he could not determine which. Bose was both. Performing sincerity. Sincere. The two things had fused, so complete that Mazumdar could not find the seam. He was not sure Bose could either. He was not sure it mattered and he was not sure that didn't matter, and the indifference wasn't the most frightening thing about the man sitting across from him cleaning his spectacles on his tie in a room in Berlin at ten o'clock at night.

Watching Bose clean his spectacles, Mazumdar understood, Bose was lonely. Not politically isolated, he was surrounded by staff, by followers, by the machinery of the Free India Centre. But lonely, a man who had committed his life to a principle that requires him to collaborate with men he despises, in a country not his own, while the country he loves is three thousand miles away.

"I sympathise with your circumstances," Bose said, putting the spectacles back on. The voice was again the public voice, soft, authoritative. "I have been fighting the British for the last fifteen years. I know what it is like to be a prisoner, as you do."

"You are not a prisoner," Mazumdar said. Bose looked at him. The lamp light caught the lenses and for a moment the eyes were invisible.

"Aren't I?" The question hung. Outside, Berlin was dark. The blackout was complete. No sound from the Tiergarten, no birds, no traffic, nothing.

Bose walked to the window. He stood with his back to Mazumdar and said, not turning, "Do you remember the Hooghly in October?"

The Hooghly was not Mazumdar's river, his was the Phalgu at Gaya, the river that vanished, but he had seen the Hooghly as a student in Calcutta, crossing the Howrah Bridge in the early morning, the water below carrying boats and flowers and the remains of the previous night's prayers.

"I remember," he said. "I used to swim in it," Bose said. "Before the politics. Before any of this. My brothers and I. The current was strong and we were not strong and we swam anyway." He was still facing the window. His reflection was faint in the glass, the spectacles, the bald head, the outline of someone who had once been a boy in a river. "I have not been in a river in four years."

Mazumdar had not been in a river in longer than that. The last time, the Phalgu, perhaps, before he left for London. The water warm and shallow and his mother watching from the ghat.

"Do you know Nahoum's?" Bose said. "On New Market." Every Bengali who had spent time in Calcutta knew Nahoum's, the Jewish bakery in the old market, the glass cases of pastries, the smell of butter and sugar that hit you three shops before you arrived. He had bought a fruit cake for his landlady at Christmas and the cake had been excellent.

"I bought my last proper cake there," Bose said. "Before the disguise. Before Peshawar. A plum cake. I ate it on the train and I thought, this is the last cake. And it was." He paused. "The Germans have good bread. They have terrible cake."

"My mother makes *sandesh*," Bose said. He turned from the window. He was almost smiling. "When I left India, when I put on the Pathan disguise and walked out of my house in Calcutta and did not tell her where I was going, the last thing I ate was a piece of *sandesh* she had made that morning. I did not know it would be the last. You never know. You eat the sweet and you leave, the taste of it is in your mouth on the train and in Afghanistan and in Moscow and then one day you are in Berlin and the taste is gone and you cannot remember when it left."

Mazumdar thought of the fish with mustard he had eaten that afternoon. The taste was still in his mouth. He swallowed.

The fish with mustard. The Bengali moving between them all afternoon. His mother.

"When did you last eat your mother's cooking?" Bose asked.

"Nineteen thirty-eight." "Four years." "Four years." Bose sat down. The formality was entirely gone now. Two Bengali men in a room in Berlin talking about their mothers' cooking at nine o'clock at night with a war outside and a disagreement between them that neither could resolve and neither wanted to abandon.

"She will be worried about you," Bose said. "She does not know where I am." "No. She knows you are somewhere. And she is worried. That is what mothers do. They worry in the direction of their sons and the worry arrives even if the address is wrong."

Mazumdar almost smiled. His face held. Something shifted behind his eyes, what in a different man would have been a smile and Bose saw it and Bose, for the first time all day, laughed. A short sound. Not loud. Something remembered catching him off guard.

"We are ridiculous," Bose said. "Two Bengalis arguing about the British Empire in the middle of Berlin. If my mother could see me she would ask if I had eaten."

"Mine would check my weight." "Has she always?" "She is the reason I became a doctor. So that I could tell her, with medical authority, that I was adequately nourished."

Bose laughed again. Longer this time. The laughter stopped. Bose poured the cold tea. He poured it for both of them without asking. Mazumdar drank it without complaint. It was terrible. Neither of them mentioned it. Outside, Berlin was dark.

V

It was past midnight. The lamp had been burning for hours and the room had contracted around it, the walls receding into shadow, the table between them reduced to a circle of light containing two cups, two pairs of hands, the ashtray Bose had been using, the lamp itself. Mazumdar's eyes were dry. He blinked. The room had been heated too long, automatic, also a way of not looking at Bose while Bose said the thing that Bose had been building toward all evening.

"Tell me, Doctor." The voice was very quiet now. Stripped of rhetoric, stripped of strategy, twelve hours of persuading, and he knew he had failed and is making the last attempt because the attempt was owed. "When you return to that castle. And they make you cook curry for them again, while they plan escapes without you. And they exclude you from the tunnel committees because your skin is the wrong colour. And they look through you at dinner. Tell me, when all of that resumes, and you are lying in your bunk in the dark, will you think about the honour of your British oath? Or will you think about this room?"

The question landed. The castle. The rectangle of sky from his window. Ellingham's fingers finding him in the dark of the washroom. The curry, turmeric under his fingernails, laughter from below, the performance of Indianness for men who saw Indianness as entertainment. The cooler for addressing a German officer in German. The escape committee excluding him from the French tunnel. Eating alone in the mess while the other officers discussed the cricket.

And then — nothing. Not a thought. Not even the absence of a thought. A gap. The place where the answer should have been was empty and the emptiness was not eloquent, was not meaningful and was simply empty, and he sat in it and could not —

"I will think about both," he said. Bose looked at him for a long time. The lamp between them. The cold tea. The ashtray with its column of ash.

Neither of them moved. The building was silent. Somewhere a pipe ticked as the heating cooled. The sound was small, regular. It did not belong to the conversation and did not care.

The ache in his lower back. The stiffness in his knees. The weariness that comes from sustained attention, the mind held at high function for twelve hours without rest. The coffee wearing off. The day settling into him, the food, the argument, the laughter, the wound he had made and the wound Bose had made and the Bengali and the cold tea and all of it sinking where it would remain, undissolved, for the rest of his life.

Bose's cigarette had burned to the filter. He stubbed it out. The ashtray was full. He had not noticed them being smoked.

The lamp flickered. The oil was low. The light shifted, a small dimming, barely perceptible, but enough to change the quality of the shadows on Bose's face. We are running out of light.

"Think it over," Bose said. "We will meet again in the morning."

He stood. He extended his hand. The handshake was the same as the first, dry, firm.

Bose walked him to the door. At the door he stopped. The corridor beyond was dim, long, smelling of floor polish. At the far end, a window through which the blacked-out city was a darkness indistinguishable from the corridor's own darkness.

"I have been fighting for fifteen years," Bose said. "I have given up everything. My home. My career. The woman I —" He stopped.

"Good night, Doctor," Bose said. Mazumdar walked down the corridor. His footsteps on the polished floor were the only sound. The building was dark, the offices on either side closed, the doors shut, the Free India Centre emptied of everyone except the two men it had spent the day trying to bring together. A coat on a hook near the stairwell. Someone had left it. The sleeve hung at an angle.

At the stairwell he heard the door close — far down the corridor, with the soft click of a mechanism designed to be reopened, and the sound of it stayed with him as the coffee had stayed with him, a physical residue of a room he was leaving and could never entirely leave.

He did not look back. But he knew, without looking, that the door was not locked.

THE SLEEPLESS NIGHT

Chapter 12

I

The sheets were clean.

This was the first thing and for a long time it was the only thing. He lay on his back in the dark with his arms at his sides and his eyes open and the sheets were clean and smooth and cool against his skin and the sensation was so unfamiliar that his body did not know what to do with it. At Colditz the sheets were changed fortnightly, smelling of previous occupants and institutional soap that removed neither smell nor memory. These sheets smelled of nothing. Of cotton and laundry soap and the faint chemical sweetness of a room recently cleaned. The absence of other men.

The mattress held him. Not as the Colditz mattress held him, a thin pad on iron slats that found his spine within minutes and held it accountable for every hour spent horizontal. This mattress gave. It received his weight and distributed it and the distribution was so even that for the first few minutes he could not feel the bed beneath him at all, only the sensation of being held, which was the sensation of not being in pain, which was a sensation he had forgotten was available.

The room was dark. Not the dark of the castle — that dark was populated, it contained the breathing of men on either side and above and below, the coughing, the shifting, the sound of a man pretending to sleep. This dark was empty. It contained only him. The silence in it was the silence of a room where no one else existed.

Plumbing. Water moving through pipes in the wall behind his head, a distant, irregular sound, the building's circulation. And beyond the plumbing, the city. Distant. A vehicle. A siren, brief, far away. Berlin at night, blacked out and enormous, continuing without him.

The taste of the coffee was still in his mouth. He had brushed his teeth, the toothbrush provided, the toothpaste German, a brand he did not recognise, and the coffee had survived. It sat at the back of his tongue, dark and bitter, the last residue of the room downstairs.

Eyes closed. His body was ready for sleep. He could feel the readiness, the heaviness in his limbs, the slowing of his breath, the loosening of the muscles across his shoulders that signals the transition from waking to unconscious. The body had been given everything it required: food, warmth, a horizontal surface, clean linen, silence. It was ready to stop.

His mind was not.

II

Bose's voice arrived first. As presence, the voice itself in the room, as though the walls had absorbed it during the day and were releasing it now into the dark.

You have described a symptom and called it a principle. Onto his side. The sheets moved with him, frictionless, accommodating. The pillow was cool against his cheek.

That is a distinction the system encourages you to make. Not in order. The sentences arrived by weight, the heaviest first, the ones that had landed hardest, the ones that had left marks.

When you return to that castle. And they make you cook curry for them again.

The curry. The kitchen at Colditz. The turmeric under his fingernails that would not come off for two days. The laughter from the dining room below, not unkind, not deliberately cruel, the laughter of men enjoying a meal prepared by a man they had not invited to share it. He had stood in the kitchen with the smell of cumin on his hands and listened to the laughter and the listening had been,

What? What had the listening been? He reached for the word and the word was not there. Not anger. Not humiliation. Something between them, lower, quieter, with no word attached.

Shoulder blades against the mattress. The ceiling was invisible in the dark. He stared at where it would be.

The fish with mustard. The taste was still in his mouth. What he remembered most vividly from twelve hours with the most significant Indian revolutionary alive was not the politics, not the strategic case. It was the fish. The sharp yellow heat of mustard. The body remembering Bengal before the mind consented.

The scalpel is neutral. The hand that gives you the scalpel is not.

Eyes closed. Opened. The dark was the same.

III

The washroom. Ellingham's voice, *That bloody Mazumdar is a spy. He's going to Berlin.*

My blood tingled from my feet to my head. I'll kill you. You don't know what I've gone through. He lay in the clean sheets and the memory was in his fists. He could feel the impact of Ellingham's jaw in his right hand, the knuckles reporting, the metacarpals carrying the shock, two things simultaneously. Shame, a doctor does not beat a man on a washroom floor. And release, closer to the feeling of a valve being opened, the pressure finding at last an exit, and the fist had felt like the first honest thing his body had done in two years.

And beneath the washroom, another voice, older, from another room, another country. The Panzer commander climbing down from the turret outside Neufchâtel. Perfect English. *I'm sorry. I'm afraid you won't reach Boulogne. And please, don't try to escape.* Please.

The German had said please. The enemy had said please while the allies said Jumbo.

It is the oath's cost. And you are paying it.

IV

His father's voice was different. It did not arrive as presence. It arrived as weight, a force that had always been in the room, beneath the floor, load-bearing, the foundation on which the building stood.

Duty, loyalty, morality, sincerity, stick to these principles and you won't go far wrong.

Said at the dinner table. After the reading of *The Times*, the imported copy, days old by the time it reached Gaya, the news already history by the time his father folded the paper and set it beside his plate. Said with warmth. Not the warmth of indulgence, someone who believed what he was saying so completely that the belief radiated from him as heat radiates from a body. The warmth was the conviction.

His father's hands on the table. The hands he had watched in the surgery, the kerosene lamp turning everything amber, the wrists turning inside a patient, the pause before the incision. Those hands had held the knife. The knife had been neutral, the same knife for the British officer with the septic wound and the farmer's wife with the tumour, and the neutrality had been a principle enacted. His father had never said: I treat all patients equally. He had simply treated all patients equally. The young Biren had watched. The watching had been the lesson, the lesson had been so thoroughly absorbed that it had become invisible.

A gentleman's word is his bond. Not a British principle. Not an Indian principle. A principle. His father had received it from the British, believed it, and transmitted it to his son. The belief survived transmission intact because the man had embodied it so completely the son could not separate principle from man. To reject the principle would be to reject the father. And the father was the one person in

Mazumdar's life who had never looked at him and seen a colour. Who had looked at him and seen a son, then a student, and then a colleague, and the progression had been natural and the naturalness had been the gift.

Carbolic acid and kerosene, the surgery in Gaya. And the sweetness of infected tissue that you learn to identify before you learn to treat. His father moving between patients with the economy of forty years' practice, still careful because carelessness in this work is not a lapse but a death. The patients waiting on the bench outside, some seated, some lying on the ground, some accompanied by families who had walked from villages whose names Mazumdar had never learned. His father knowing every name. The patients were people and people have names and a doctor who forgets this has forgotten the thing that makes the medicine worth practising.

Stick to these principles. In the dark his father's voice held him the way the mattress held him, from beneath, distributed, so even that you could not feel where the support began and the self ended.

Bose had called it a cage. *You are choosing to remain in it.* And the two voices, Bose's and his father's, occupied the same dark, the same room, the same pillow, the same clean sheets that smelled of nothing and held him in a comfort that was either kindness or strategy and he could not determine which, the determination required a vantage point outside both voices and there was no vantage point outside both voices because one was his inheritance and the other was his experience and between inheritance and experience there is no neutral ground.

V

Three o'clock, perhaps. Four. The hour when the circadian rhythm reaches its trough, core temperature lowest, cortisol not yet rising, the mind in the state between sleep and waking where the doors that the conscious mind keeps closed swing open on their own. The thought arrived.

No sleep. The plumbing had stopped. The city was silent. The thought: The oath is not honour. The oath is erasure. It did not arrive as a sentence. It arrived as — he did not know what it arrived as. Not a thought. Not a feeling. Something beneath both. A shift in the ground. The sensation of a floor that has been solid revealing itself to be a surface over a depth, the depth always there, the surface always thin, and the thinness now, at this hour, in this bed, in this building in Berlin with Bose's door still unlocked somewhere below him, suddenly apparent.

By keeping his word to men who did not recognise his humanity he was not preserving his integrity. He was —

He reached for the clinical vocabulary. The vocabulary that had contained everything — the fear at Kassel, the isolation at Colditz, the rage on the washroom floor, the admiration for Bose, the food, the loneliness, the rectangle of sky — the vocabulary that had given him a framework for every experience of the past two years, that had allowed him to observe his own suffering with the detachment of a man reading a chart, that had been his instrument and his armour and his way of remaining himself in circumstances designed to unmake him.

The vocabulary was not there. Because the gaze was the oath. He understood this now. The clinical training and the military oath were the same submission. Both were voluntary entries into a British system.

Both had given him tools, the scalpel, the commission, the framework, the vocabulary, and the tools had been excellent and the excellence had been the price, the excellence had replaced whatever had been there before the training began. His father's pause before the incision. The hand resting on the body. The registrar's look. The pause he had never repeated.

What was there before? What had Biren known before the Royal College taught him what to see?

Unknown. The not-knowing was the answer and the answer was the Crack and the Crack was —

The instrument was the disease. The thing he would use to examine the wound was the thing that had made the wound and the recursion was complete, the vocabulary was not there and —

His hands went cold. The clinical mind knew cold as a physiological fact, vasoconstriction, blood redirected to the central organs. The knowing did not prevent it, the body observed and understood and still refusing to obey, still performing the cold, still proving that the instrument was not the instrumentalist.

Silence. His own breathing. The pipes. The thought sank. It went under the way a river goes under in Bihar, still moving in the dark beneath the sand, still flowing, giving no sign.

Down. He pushed it down.

VI

The light came slowly. Grey first, the window emerging from the dark, a paler rectangle in the wall, the curtains becoming visible as fabric rather than shadow. Then a colourlessness between night and morning. The room surfacing around him in pieces, the chair, the table, the glass of water he had not drunk, the door.

No sleep. His eyes were dry and the dryness was familiar, the same dryness from the room downstairs, the twelve hours of open eyes, the blinking that was automatic and insufficient. His body ached from stillness. Seven hours in a bed that was too comfortable, the muscles held in a tension that the comfort could not reach, the tension was not in the muscles.

Upright now. The sheets fell away from his chest. The skin where the sacred thread had once rested, from left shoulder to right hip, the cotton thread received at Upanayana, lost at Kassel during the delousing, never replaced, the skin there was no different from the skin around it. There was nothing to see. There had not been anything to see for two years. He did not touch the place. He did not look at it. His lips moved, the first syllable of the Gayatri, the dawn prayer taught at the ceremony where the thread was given, *Om*, and stopped.

His mouth closed around the silence where the second syllable should have been. He put his feet on the floor.

The floor was cold. German cold: hard, institutional, coming up through the boards into his bare soles, the grain of the wood pressing into the soft skin of his arches. Nothing like the stone floors at Colditz, which had been cold for four hundred years and would be cold for four hundred more. This cold was recent. Everything in this building was temporary.

On his feet. At the window. Berlin in early morning, the Tiergarten below, the trees visible now, the paths empty, a low mist sitting on the grass. Beyond the park, buildings, government buildings, ministry buildings, the architecture of a regime that would, if Bose was right about one thing, not last. The city was quiet. A milk cart, perhaps, somewhere. The sound of a city that has not yet decided to begin its day.

He would say no. The knowledge was in him the way the coffee had been in him, a residue left behind by the night, by the hours of thinking, by the two voices arguing in the dark. Not a resolution. The Crack was still there. The thought that the oath was erasure had not been answered. It had been pushed underground. It was still moving beneath the surface. It would surface again, the certainty was clinical, the certainty of a condition seen before, and when it surfaced again it would be stronger because unresolved things do not weaken in the dark. They strengthen.

But the oath was his. Not Britain's. His. Water on his face. Warm. Of course it was. Towel, white, soft. He folded it and placed it on the rail with a precision that was automatic. He was a man who folded towels precisely. He was a man who kept his word. These were not different things. The same discipline, the same inheritance, the same code. Chronic, managed, never cured.

He dressed. The clothes they had provided, clean, pressed, civilian, hung on the chair. He put on his own uniform. It was creased from the journey, smelling of the train and of Colditz and of a man who has worn the same clothes for three days. The smell was his. The uniform was his. The King's Commission on the shoulder was his.

Buttons fastened. Collar straightened. He looked at the door.

Somewhere below, in his office or his private quarters, Bose was awake or would soon be awake and would be waiting for an answer. The answer would disappoint him. The disappointment would be genuine, because the recruitment had been genuine, the argument genuine, the food and the Bengali and every moment of the twelve hours. None of it had been false. Bose had meant every word. That was the thing. That was what made the refusal cost what it cost.

Door open. The corridor was bright with morning light. At the far end, a window, and through the window the Tiergarten in early sun, the mist burning off, the city beginning.

Toward the stairs. His footsteps on the polished floor. The same corridor he had walked in darkness seven hours ago, after the door had closed with the soft click of a mechanism designed to be reopened. The door had not been locked then. It was not locked now. It would never be locked. Bose did not lock doors. Bose left them open and let you decide.

Down the stairs. He would say no, and the no would be the most expensive word of his life, and the expense would not diminish. He descended the stairs.

THE REFUSAL

Chapter 13

I

Bose was already at the table.

The breakfast had been laid out with the same care as the dinner: eggs, toast, fruit, a pot of coffee that filled the room with its particular warmth. Bose sat behind the food as he had sat behind the desk, with the posture of total occupation.

"Doctor. Sit." Same chair. Same table. But the room had changed overnight because he had changed overnight and the change was in his chest, not the Crack, not the old fracture, but a clarity. A decision that had already been made, unspoken, somewhere in the hours between two and five, in the body's own parliament where votes are cast without language.

Bose poured coffee. The gesture was unhurried. He poured as if the morning contained no urgency.

"You look tired." "I did not sleep well."

Bose smiled. "Good," he said. "A man who sleeps well after such a conversation has not understood it."

II

They did not discuss it immediately. They ate. Bose talked about Calcutta, the house on Elgin Road, the garden, the jasmine that bloomed in January. He talked about his mother's cooking. Deliberate, Mazumdar understood, the body first, the argument second. Feed the man. Remind him of home.

The eggs were good. The toast was warm. The coffee was real coffee, not the grey institutional liquid of Colditz, and the goodness was argument enough.

Then Bose set down his cup. The setting-down was precise, cup aligned with saucer, saucer aligned with table edge.

"Will you join us, Doctor?" Quiet, the room. The Tiergarten through the window, winter trees, grey sky, a woman walking a dog on the path below.

"No." The word was smaller than he had expected. Two letters. A sound that lasted less than a second.

Bose did not move. His hands remained on the table. "May I ask why?" "The oath." "The oath," Bose repeated. Not a question. A weighing. "I swore allegiance to the King. When I accepted the commission. I swore it, not a formality. I understood what I was swearing and I cannot unswear it because the men who gave me the commission are unworthy of it."

Bose's silence, the silence of a man listening with his whole body, as the best diagnosticians listen, not for the words but for what the words are built on.

"You understand," Bose said, "that this oath was given to a King who considers you a subject. Not a citizen."

"Yes." "And that the army in which you serve considers you inferior by birth."

"Yes." "And that you have been imprisoned in a castle where your fellow British officers refused to help you escape because your face is brown."

"Yes." "And still the oath." "And still the oath." Bose leaned back. The chair creaked. For a moment he was not the leader, not the revolutionary. He was a man who had heard something he recognised.

"You are an unusual man, Doctor." "I am a man who made a promise." Bose stood. The light from the window caught his spectacles and for a moment his eyes were invisible behind two discs of white.

"I have chosen my way, and you have chosen yours. Goodbye and good luck." An extended hand.

Mazumdar shook it. The right hand. The hand that had struck Ellingham and now held Subhas Chandra Bose's palm, gentle on both sides, the gentleness of two men who had understood each other completely and would never agree.

He was at the door when Bose's voice followed him: "When you change your mind, we will be here."

III

The car came at noon. The same guard, the same driver. Berlin passed in reverse.

Not first class, the return train. Wooden benches. Two guards. A window that did not open. He had been offered and had refused. The refusal moved him from one category to another, from asset to problem. The category change was in the bench and the guards and the sealed window.

Past Leipzig, the aching stopped. He noticed it, flexing the fingers, finding the joints loose, the swelling reduced. Three days since Ellingham. The body heals. The body does not know about oaths.

Colditz by evening. The castle on its rock. He walked through the gate. The courtyard was dark. The windows were lit. Engles would be inside, and the meeting would end with a nod and no questions.

The castle received him. The stones were cold. He was home, and the home was a prison, and the prison was the place he had chosen.

THE COST

Chapter 14

I

He walked through the gate and the gate closed behind him, the same sound it had made when he arrived, iron on stone, final, but the finality now had a different quality. Before, the gate had closed him in. Now it closed him back.

The courtyard was cold. June, but cold, the castle's cold, the stone's cold, the cold that travelled up through the soles of his shoes. His hands were still in his pockets from the train ride, and he kept them there.

Dark, the courtyard. Figures moved behind lit windows. He could feel the watching begin before he reached the stairs, the information travelling ahead of him, the castle's nervous system faster than his legs. *He's back. The Indian is back from Berlin.*

Engles was waiting in the corridor. He did not ask. He looked, the thin face searching Mazumdar's face with careful attention. What had happened in Berlin would not be spoken tonight or perhaps ever. The not-speaking was survival.

"You're back." "I'm back." "And?" "And I am still what I was." Engles nodded. The nod was slow and contained a relief that surprised Mazumdar, a relief that said Engles had considered the possibility that the man who returned would not be the man who left, and that the considering had cost him something.

They sat in the corridor and it was enough.

II

After Berlin, a narrowing. Stanhope summoned him the next morning. The SBO's office, such as it was, a repurposed room with a desk and the authority of rank, was cold. Stanhope did not offer a chair.

"Well?" "I refused, Colonel." "Refused what, exactly?" He told him. Not everything, not the fish with mustard, not the Bengali, not the laughter about mothers, not the way Bose's voice had made the room on Lichtenstein Allee feel like a room in Calcutta. He told him the operational facts, the offer, the refusal, the terms.

Stanhope listened with the expression of a man sorting information into categories, useful, dangerous, irrelevant, the sorting visible in his eyes.

"Didn't he want you after all?"

"Oh yes, he wanted me all right, and I would very much have liked to accept his offer to join him. He's such a wonderful man." The office was cold. His hands were at his sides. They did not clench. They did not open. They hung, the fingers extended, the palms facing the wall, the hands of a man holding something so carefully that the holding looked like empty air. "But then I couldn't, could I?"

"Why ever not?" "Because I hold a British commission, and I therefore owe my loyalty to the King, whatever my political views may be."

Stanhope's expression did not change. He would file the information and never discuss it.

"Very well. You should know that we will be watching you closely."

"I expected nothing else, sir." He stood. At the door he turned. "Look, Colonel, I'm going to escape one day." "Well, don't expect us to give you anything, maps or money."

“It’s what I expected, sir. You will hear from me.”

He left the office. The corridor was stone and the sound of his footsteps arrived before his feet had finished making them. Behind him the door closed. The corridor was full of other doors, all closed, and behind each door was information, the war, the castle’s secrets, the plans that did not include him. The footsteps continued. The sound of the castle’s machinery, the guards moving between sections, the radio playing in an unseen room, the mechanisms of confinement operating at every level, every level containing a sound, every sound saying, the castle continues.

Berlin had changed things. The other prisoners knew he had been taken. They did not know why. Rumours moved through the castle, he had been offered something, he had refused something, the Germans had singled him out, and the rumours changed the looking. Before Berlin, the looking had been simple, the brown face, the wrong face, the face that did not belong. After Berlin, the looking acquired a new layer. He was not merely the Indian. He was the Indian who had been singled out by the Germans, taken somewhere, returned. The singling-out was suspicious. The return was suspicious. A man who goes to Berlin and comes back is either a collaborator or a marked man and neither category invited warmth.

Back to the kitchen. Back to the pot. The pot was heavy, cast iron, older than he was, its weight in his hands familiar now after months of lifting it. He sat in the courtyard during the permitted hours and felt the walls press closer. Each day was a contraction. The courtyard’s twenty-seven metres became twenty-six, twenty-five. The attic ceiling lowered. The kitchen walls leaned in.

At night the Phalgu. The river going underground. The water still moving beneath the dry bed. He thought about it at night when the bunk was hard and the window showed stars that were not his stars and the silence of the castle pressed against him like a second confinement, the silence of men who had decided he was not to be trusted, which was worse.

He began to think about escape. Not the escape the committee had refused him, the tunnel, the disguise, the forged papers, the collective enterprise of white men helping white men through white countries. A different escape. His own. An escape that required no committee and no approval and no one's help. An escape that used the only leverage a prisoner has when every other leverage has been removed.

The body. The idea came to him in the kitchen. He was peeling potatoes. The same motion, the same blade, the same pile growing in the same tin. His knuckles still ached from Berlin, the joint swollen slightly where Ellingham had punched him on the transport, and the aching was a small thing beneath the larger ache of everything else, but it was there, reminding the hands of what the fists had done, and the idea arrived without drama, as diagnoses sometimes arrive, the pattern resolving with a quiet click, the last symptom falling into place.

He would stop eating. Clinical, the logic. A hunger strike would force a transfer. The Germans could not allow an officer to die of self-imposed starvation, the Geneva Convention, the Red Cross, the appearances. They would move him. They would move him to a camp with lower security and Indian prisoners and the possibility of escape that Colditz did not offer. The hunger strike was not a protest. It was a strategy.

He peeled another potato. The blade moved. The skin curled.

Precision. He would need to monitor his own vitals, heart rate, blood pressure by palpation, cognitive function by self-assessment. He would need to know exactly how far he could push before the body began to fail irreversibly. He would need, in other words, to be both the patient and the doctor, the experiment and the experimenter.

He set down the blade. The potato was white and smooth in his hand.

February twelfth. He would begin on February twelfth. Two days earlier, on the tenth, Gandhi had begun his own hunger strike, his fifteenth, the news arriving through the hidden radio, circulating through the castle with the velocity of information that cannot be verified. His political idol, detained without charges by the British, refusing food in an Indian prison. And now he would refuse food in a German one. The symmetry was not calculated. It was inherited, the knowledge, deep in the body, that this was how an Indian fought when every other weapon had been taken.

THE FAST

Chapter 15

I

Day one was nothing.

He did not eat breakfast. He did not eat lunch. He did not eat dinner. The not-eating was simple — a closing of the mouth, a turning-away, the body's compliance with the mind's instruction. By evening the hunger was a mild pressure behind the sternum, nothing more. He drank tea, the cup warm in his hands, the warmth travelling through the ceramic into his palms, the only heat the body would receive today. He could feel the liquid travel the length of his oesophagus and arrive in the empty stomach, where it sat, alone, the stomach walls contracting around it with a puzzled persistence. The body had reserves. The body had been preparing for scarcity since the convoy at Étaples, since the march, since the years of institutional food that never quite satisfied. The body knew how to wait.

He told Ferguson on the second morning.

"You know, Ferguson, I have decided not to stay here any longer."

Ferguson looked at him. The look was long and contained the calculation of a man assessing whether his friend had gone mad.

"I'm prepared to bet you that I shall not be here in a fortnight."

Ferguson said nothing. The look intensified, the eyes narrowing, the mouth setting, the Irishman's face performing the work of comprehension without the assistance of speech.

"You think I am joking, don't you, Fergy? Well, I will show you that you are wrong."

Ferguson sat on the edge of the bunk. The sitting was heavy, heavy, what he was hearing was strategy.

"You'll need watching." "I'll need leaving alone." "You'll need watching and you'll get it." Ferguson's voice was a door closing, final, without anger, the Irish consonants carrying a weight that had nothing to do with the words and everything to do with the man. He would watch. He would not be persuaded otherwise. The decision was made in the same moment as the statement and the two were inseparable.

II

Day three. The hunger deepened.

It moved from the sternum to the abdomen, a hollow ache that was absence, the body registering the space where food should be. He drank water. The water filled the stomach temporarily, a lie the body saw through within minutes, the stomach contracting around nothing, the water absorbed and the absence returning.

Self-monitoring. Pulse: sixty-eight. Cognitive function, intact. Muscle tone: unchanged. He recorded the numbers in his head: no paper, no pen, the record kept in the same place where the medical knowledge lived, beneath the English, beneath the institutional language, in the place where the doctor operated even when the man was failing.

By day four the other prisoners noticed. The kitchen was a public space and his absence from it was visible, the cook who did not eat, the Indian who sat in his bunk while the others filed to meals. The noticing produced the usual range: curiosity, indifference, a few glances that held what looked like concern. The phrase circulated by evening, *Jumbo is doing a Gandhi*, and the phrase was said with the same tone as every other remark about him: dismissive, amused, the tone of men who had classified his existence as entertainment and saw no reason to reclassify it now.

He did not know, could not have known, in a castle without newspapers or wireless, that four days before he stopped eating, the man who had asked him to choose had made his own departure. Subhas Chandra Bose had left Kiel on February eighth aboard U-180, a German submarine bound for the Indian Ocean, carrying with him the dream of an Indian army that would march on Delhi under a different flag. The man who had served fish with mustard and spoken Bengali across a table on Lichtenstein Allee was now beneath the Atlantic, moving east through the dark water, and the man who had refused him was in a castle in Saxony, moving inward through the dark of his own body. Two men who had sat across a table eight months ago were now both going underground, one in a submarine, one in a hunger strike, and neither man knew about the other's descent.

When he heard it, he smiled. "I know what I am doing," he said. "We shall see what we shall see."

The senior British officer came on day five. He stood at the end of the bunk with his hands behind his back and his face arranged in the expression of official concern that senior officers deploy when confronted with a problem that falls outside the operational manual.

"Mazumdar. You're not eating." "No, sir." "Is this a protest?" "It is a request for transfer." "Transfer is not within my authority." "No, sir. But it is within the authority of the men whose attention my condition will attract if it continues."

The colonel's face changed. The change was small, a tightening around the eyes, a recalibration, and in the change Mazumdar saw recognition. The colonel understood. The hunger strike was not directed at him. It was directed past him, over his head, at the German command structure that had brought Mazumdar to Berlin and beaten him for refusing, returned him to a castle where he had no allies and no escape and no future. The hunger strike was addressed to that structure, and the structure would have to answer.

"I cannot order you to eat." "No, sir." The colonel left. His footsteps echoed in the corridor: precise, measured, the footsteps of a man retreating from a situation he could not control.

III

Day seven. Heart rate fifty-eight.

Glycogen gone, burned through in the first seventy-two hours, the liver's emergency reserve consumed, and the body had turned to fat. He could feel the transition in the fatigue: a deeper, slower weariness that sat in the muscles and the joints and the spaces behind the eyes. Ketosis. The breath acquiring the faint sweetness of acetone that he had smelled on diabetic patients in the Royal College wards.

He lay on the bunk. The ceiling was low and grey and familiar. The cracks in the plaster formed a pattern he had memorised in the first weeks and now saw without seeing, the pattern as much a part of the room as the walls.

At noon the smell came through the walls. The kitchen. Someone was cooking — the heat and the fat, the boiling water produced a smell that entered the corridor and climbed the stairs and found him. The smell was not hunger. The smell was the kitchen, the stove he had stood at for months, the pots he had scraped clean, the one thing he had done in this castle that required skill rather than endurance. The hunger strike had taken that from him too. He had given up the making of food, the one act that used his hands as a doctor's hands rather than a prisoner's. The smell stayed. He turned his face to the wall.

Ferguson came three times a day, morning, midday, evening, with water and the silent presence of witness. To be watched in this was to be held accountable, the gaze itself a kind of warmth that did not ask. Ferguson's presence said: *I see you. I see what this is costing. You will not do this alone.*

The German camp doctor visited on day eight. He took Mazumdar's pulse and blood pressure and listened to his chest with the competent hurry of a man performing a duty he wished someone else had been assigned.

"You should eat, Herr Doktor."

"I know what prolonged fasting does. I am a Fellow of the Royal College of Surgeons. I know precisely what is happening to my body and I am choosing it."

The doctor closed his bag. "I will report your condition." "Please do."

IV

Day ten. Heart rate fifty.

Fat reserves diminishing. He could feel the body's next transition beginning, the shift from fat to muscle, from stored energy to structural tissue, the body beginning to consume itself. The weakness was no longer in the muscles alone. It was in the bones, in the tendons, in the connective tissue that held the body together. Standing required effort. Walking to the washroom was a project that required planning, the route, the handholds, the places where the wall could bear his weight.

Ferguson brought water. The water was warm. Ferguson had heated it somehow, in the kitchen, and the warmth was a kindness that Mazumdar received without comment because commenting would have broken something neither of them could afford to break.

Around him, the castle watched. He could feel it, the awareness of a building full of men who had ignored him for months now tracking his deterioration with the attention they had previously reserved for escape committees and tunnel measurements. The hunger strike had done what the cooking and the cleaning and the surviving had not, it had made him visible.

THE EDGE

Chapter 16

I

Day eleven. Heart rate forty-six.

He counted it with his fingers on his own wrist, the way he had counted it every morning since the strike began. The fingers were still capable. The radial pulse was still palpable. The number, when it arrived, was a number he could hold in his mind and compare against the numbers from previous days and the comparison told him what he already knew, the heart was slowing. The heart was doing what hearts do when the body has consumed its glycogen and its fat and has begun on its own muscle. The heart is a muscle.

Top bunk, back of the attic, farthest from the window. The light from the window reached him late in the afternoon and left early, a diminishment he felt but did not measure. The hollows above his clavicles where bone pressed against skin with a prominence that was not normal. Subcutaneous fat depleted. Temporal wasting visible. The blanket was rough. He had not noticed the roughness before the strike and now the roughness was information, the nerve endings closer to the surface, the padding between skin and sensation reduced. The body was eating itself in the order the body always eats itself, glycogen, adipose, muscle, and the order was textbook, the textbook was in his mind and the mind was the last thing the body would eat.

Wool and pigeons and the sourness of men who are not well. He had been one of these men for eleven days. The smell was his now.

Ferguson came every four hours. Water and words. The water Mazumdar drank. The words he sometimes heard, sometimes did not. They arrived from a distance that was increasing, the distance between the world Ferguson occupied and the world Mazumdar was entering, at the speed of metabolism.

A cigarette between fingers that had thinned, the smoke rising from a body that had nothing else to burn. The taste of tobacco on an empty stomach was a taste that belonged to no food and no country, the one act that was still entirely his.

"... must eat ... cannot continue ... Biren ..." *Biren.* The name arrived differently from the other words. From beneath them. From the place where names live, deeper than English, deeper than medicine, deeper than the castle. *Biren.* The name his father called him. His mother. The name that was first and would be last and that Ferguson used because Ferguson understood it was a recognition.

Ferguson's hands were on the bed rail. Large hands. Surgeon's hands. Useless.

"I know what I am doing." He heard himself say this, delayed, the sound arriving after the words had left his mouth. A gap. The brain consuming glucose at a rate insufficient for its usual operations and compensating by reducing what it considered non-essential. Apparently the gap between speaking and hearing oneself speak was non-essential.

II

From the other side, the Germans were watching too.

A new commandant had arrived the day after the strike began, Oberst Prawitt, replacing Glaesche, the timing a coincidence that felt like a plot. The first item on his desk was a report about an Indian doctor who had stopped eating, and the item did not improve his first impression of his new command. Messages flew between Colditz and Berlin. The bureaucracy of a hunger strike is considerable, reports, medical assessments, consultations with regional command, the paperwork of a body consuming itself, each form a record of the institution's failure to make a man eat.

Daily, the camp doctor visited. By day ten the professional neutrality had gone from his examinations, the stethoscope pressed harder than necessary against the sternum, the fingers at the wrist lingering, the German doctor's face performing a calculation Mazumdar could read because it was the calculation he would have made himself: pulse thready, blood pressure falling, peripheral oedema absent but cachexia advancing. The camp doctor's report to Prawitt was brief. The conclusion was not optimistic.

A German NCO, Unteroffizier Schädlich, who kept a diary, noted that the Indian doctor had not eaten in two weeks. Only tea. Cigarettes. Nothing else.

Three facts in a German diary. The noticing was neither hostile nor sympathetic but accurate, and the accuracy was the kindest thing anyone said about the hunger strike while it was happening. Tea and cigarettes. A man reduced to two acts, the liquid and the burning, and the two acts were the minimum, the irreducible, the body's last transactions with the material world.

An appeal to Prawitt. The Senior British Officer asked the commandant to intervene, to save the Indian doctor from himself. The word used was *little.* Was it affection? Was it diminishment? Was it both? The SBO who had never once intervened on Mazumdar's behalf during the months of the washroom and the looking and the margins was now asking the German commandant to save him, an acknowledgement that the castle had failed, the failure mutual, and the Indian doctor's starving body was the document of the failure.

III

Day twelve. Heart rate — he had counted it. The number had been there. The number was gone.

On the bunk. The ceiling was moving. Not moving. The ceiling was still. The eyes were moving. Nystagmus, involuntary, rhythmic, the vestibular system reporting motion where there was no motion because the vestibular system was hungry too. Hunger makes the instruments lie.

The cold. Not the cold of the castle — that cold came from outside, from stone and Saxon winter. This cold came from inside. Core temperature dropping. The body withdrawing heat from the periphery to protect the organs, the triage the body performs when the body is the disaster. His fingers were cold. His toes. The thin skin over his temples. The centre still functioning. The edges being abandoned.

Bones through skin. The zygomatic arch, the orbital rim, the mandible, structures he had learned by name in an anatomy hall in London, structures that lived beneath the skin where the skin was thick enough to hide them, and the skin was no longer thick enough. His face was becoming the skull beneath his face. Clinically, the knowledge was still available. The knowing was less precise today.

Light moved across the ceiling. The light arrived. The light left. Between the arriving and the leaving, Ferguson.

Ferguson was speaking. The words arrived in fragments. Eyes closed. Behind them the dark was different from the dark of open eyes in a dark room. This dark had texture. This dark moved.

III-A

His father's hands.

They arrived without announcement. His father's hands in the surgery in Gaya, the hands that held the scalpel as his hands held the scalpel, the grip identical because the grip had been taught, hand over hand, the boy's fingers guided by the man's fingers, the boy learning not the technique but the quality of attention that preceded the technique, the pause before the incision, the breath held, the hand resting on the body for a moment before the cutting began, not hesitation but greeting, the doctor's hand acknowledging the body it was about to open.

Never forget what you are, how you were brought up, what good luck you had.

Bengali. The language surfacing as the English receded, the English required cognitive function no longer available at the rate the brain was consuming glucose. The Bengali was deeper. Not learned but given. The language of the body before the body learned the languages the institutions required.

The surgery. The smell — carbolic and cotton and the sweetness of a wound dressed with turmeric, the old way. The sound of — what had the sound been? The kerosene lamp. The hiss of the lamp. And beneath it his father's breathing. Steady. The breathing of a man whose hands were inside another person. He could hear it. He could almost hear it. The sound arrived in pieces and the pieces did not hold.

Dressing wounds with gauze, his father then touched the bandage once, a touch that was not in any textbook, the hand of a man who believed the body was not only tissue, not only chemical.

Baba. The word surfaced. He had not thought it since Kassel. *Baba.* The man was alive. His father was alive in a house in Gaya where the mango tree grew in the courtyard and the morning surgery began at eight and between the surgeries his father sat in the chair where the light was best. Alive and present and there.

He held this the way he held the bunk rail, with whatever strength the hands had left, because the holding was what kept the world from dissolving completely. And the world was dissolving. The edges going first. The castle receding. The ceiling. The cold receding into a different cold, a warmer cold, the cold of a body that has stopped fighting.

IV

The mother.

She appeared once. On the platform at Gaya, the one the delirium had built from materials the conscious mind had locked away. The delirium had the keys.

She stood on the platform. She was wearing a white sari, the cotton plain, the border red, the specific red of *alta* dye that he had not seen since India, that arrived now with the precision of a colour the mind does not let fade, and he reached for the red as if the reaching could make it hold, as if the colour could be the thing his hands could not touch, the impossible bridge between the platform and the bunk. She was small. She was not speaking. She stood as she had stood when he left for London: erect, dry-eyed, the weeping private, the departure public. She had decided her son would not see her weep. The breach would make the leaving harder, already hard enough.

Reaching for her. The reaching was not physical, the hands on the bunk did not move. The reaching was interior, the mind extending toward the image, and the touching was not achieved. The delirium could produce the image but not the contact. The mother but not the holding.

She dissolved. The platform dissolved. The red of the border held for a moment longer than the rest, a line of colour in the dark behind his eyes, and then the red was gone, the platform was gone and the mother was gone and what remained was the Phalgu.

V

The Phalgu. Going underground.

What are you dying for? The question. The river. Surfacing. Dying in a castle in Saxony. Because British officers had called him a spy. Had told him his skin disqualified him from escape. Had made him cook curry. Had called him Jumbo. Had given him the chair near the draught. Had excluded him from the committee. And he was starving himself, a doctor, a man trained to preserve life, deliberately destroying the body he had been trained to preserve, in order to leave this place. Gandhian protest. Against the British. Inside a German prison. While remaining loyal to the British Crown.

The absurdity was total. The oath and the hunger strike were in contradiction. He kept the oath, he did not join Bose, he did not defect. And he broke the oath's hold: he forced his own transfer, he acted for himself. Both were true. The monument had a crack in it.

The river went underground again. The understanding sank, catching the light once, then gone, still flowing beneath the surface where it would flow for fifty years.

VI

Day fourteen. Or thirteen. The counting had stopped.

He lay. The ceiling. Ferguson's voice, far. Water on his lips. The water was warm. He drank. The drinking was automatic.

Bengali. He was thinking in Bengali. The English was. The English. The words. The words were.

Om Bhur Bhuvah Svah. The Gayatri. Dawn prayer. The syllables his lips had known since the Upanayana. The thread that was. Lost.

Fasting. The boy who had fasted at the Upanayana, the ritual fast, the sacred fast, the fast that preceded the thread, the boy was fasting. The body recognised the fasting as sacred. The hunger strike was. *Tapas.* The austerity. The discipline of the body for the purpose of. The purpose.

The purpose was. The ceiling was still. The eyes were still. The heart was slow. The heart. Slow.

VII

Day sixteen. A voice. German. Official. Close, the voice was close, which meant the distance had contracted, which meant something had changed.

"Die Verlegung wird genehmigt." The transfer is approved.

He opened his eyes. Ferguson was standing. Ferguson's face was relief and relief and something less nameable, someone witnessing the nearly-dying stop.

They brought broth. Thin, warm, the taste of salt and a flavour beneath the salt, the flavour arriving at the back of the throat with the faintness of a thing diluted almost to nothing.

He drank. The stomach contracted around it with the surprised urgency of an organ that had been idle for sixteen days and was now receiving what it had been designed to receive.

Won. Victory tasted like broth: thin, warm, barely there. He was alive. The heart rate was — he put his fingers on his wrist. The counting was possible again. The pulse was there. Slow. Weak. Present. A decision made in Berlin by men who calculated that an Indian officer dying on a hunger strike in a castle full of British witnesses was unacceptable propaganda, and the calculation had saved him.

Ferguson was speaking. The words arriving at the correct speed now, the gap between sound and meaning closing.

"Biren. Thank God." No thanks to God. He drank the broth. He closed his eyes. The dark was quiet. The river was underground. The heart was beating.

He would leave this place. He would walk out the front gate. He would not look back.

Or he would. Once.

THE GATE

Chapter 17

I

Day sixteen. The commandant came.

He came in the morning, when the light was thin through the window and the ward was quiet. Mazumdar was on his bunk. He had not risen in two days, the legs no longer reliable, the blood pressure insufficient for standing without the grey narrowing of vision that preceded syncope. He lay on his back with his hands on his chest and his hands were the hands of a man he did not recognise, the fingers thin, the knuckles prominent, the skin lying on the bones as cloth lies on a frame.

At the end of the bed, the commandant. He was accompanied by the camp doctor and an adjutant with a clipboard. The room was quiet and his heart, forty-four beats per minute, he counted, performed its slow, diminished work.

"Herr Doktor Mazumdar." He could hear. The hearing was adequate. The voice came through layers of fatigue, cotton layers, soft, muffling, but the words were distinct.

"You are to be transferred." The commandant's face was correct. Neither hostile nor sympathetic. The order had come from above, from this bunk through the castle through Berlin, where men in offices had weighed the cost of a dead Indian officer against the cost of a transferred one.

"An Indian camp. Bayonne. Southwest France. You will leave tomorrow."

"You should eat," the commandant said. "Tomorrow."

II

He came down from the attic that evening.

Slow, the coming-down, the stairs requiring a negotiation with gravity his legs were not prepared for, each step a decision, each landing a rest, the banisters bearing a weight they had not borne before because his hands were now load-bearing structures, the arms pulling what the legs could not push. But he came down. He emerged into the corridor and then into the common room, the men who were there saw him and the seeing produced a sound.

A cheer. Loud, sudden, filling the room. He was weak. He was gaunt. He was grinning broadly, the grin arriving on the skull-face with a brightness that was almost obscene. He had won a bet against his own body and was alive to collect.

The cheering was the first collective sound directed at him that carried neither mockery nor suspicion. The men who had called him Jumbo were cheering him because the doing had worked and the working had required a courage they recognised, the solitary courage of a man who had used the only weapon available to him and had not died.

Brief, the moment. The cheering would end and the castle would return to its hierarchies. But the moment existed. He stood in it.

Ferguson brought broth. The broth was warm and thin and it entered the stomach with a sensation he had not expected, pain. The stomach, contracted to the size of a fist after sixteen days without content, received the liquid as an insult. The cramping was immediate and fierce and he breathed through it: steady, measured, the exhalation twice the length of the inhalation.

"Slowly," Ferguson said. "I know." "I know you know. I'm saying it anyway." He drank slowly. The broth stayed. The stomach held it with the wariness of an organ that had been betrayed and was not yet ready to trust. Ferguson sat on the floor with his back against the wall and did not speak.

Minutes passed. The cramping eased. The broth settled into him, not comfort yet, but ceasefire.

"Bayonne," Ferguson said. "Bayonne." "Indian camp." "Yes." "Lower security." "Yes." Ferguson nodded. "You'll make it." "I'll try." "No. You'll make it."

III

He left on the morning of February twenty-eighth. Out through the front gates of Colditz he walked, the same gates through which he had entered more than a year ago in the back of a truck, in the dark, knowing nothing. The walking was slow. The muscles had not yet rebuilt, and the tendons were slack, and the body was a structure that required will to perform the basic operations of locomotion. But he walked. He did not ride. He walked out.

Empty, the courtyard. He had not said goodbye to anyone except Ferguson.

But two things happened before he reached the gate. Ellingham found him. The Guardsman, six foot two, the jaw Mazumdar had broken on the washroom floor, appeared at the end of the corridor and walked toward him.

"I am very sorry," Ellingham said. "I am extending an invitation to stay with me and my family after the war."

Mazumdar looked at the face. The jaw had healed. The man had not.

He shook Ellingham's hand. He said nothing. Then the escape committee. The men who had told him he could not escape with his brown skin now presented him with a brand-new arse-creeper packed tight with German banknotes. He took the tube. The banknotes would be useful. The gesture would not be forgotten.

Ferguson waited by the gate. His face in the February cold was red at the cheeks and white at the nose and the eyes were steady.

"The oath holds." "Yes." Ferguson's breath made a cloud in the February air. The cloud hung between them for a moment and then it was gone.

"Then everything else is logistics."

He walked through the gate. The February air hit his face: raw, wet, the cold finding the thinned skin at his temples and the hollow beneath his cheekbones where the hunger strike had carved away the fat. His lungs filled with air that tasted of woodsmoke and rain and open ground, a shock. The road descended. Behind him the castle rose, grey, massive, and he looked back. Once. The courtyard, the grey walls, the high windows, the arch through which he had entered more than a year ago with a shaved head and a rage he had not yet learned to name.

Then the road turned and the castle was gone. His body was thin and his pulse was slow and his muscles trembled with the effort of sitting upright. But the body was his. He had bet it and he had won — depleted, damaged, alive.

THE JUMP

Chapter 18

I

He heard them before he saw them.

South and west for two days — through Saxony, across the Rhine, through a France he had not seen since the convoy at Étaples three years ago. The country had changed. The roads were emptier. The towns were quieter. The occupation had settled into France the way a chronic illness settles into a body, the slow depletion that comes after.

Then the sound. Hindi. Punjabi. Bengali. The languages arriving through the window of the truck, overlapping, interrupting. The sound was a wall of voices, and the voices were the first Indian voices he had heard since Kassel in 1940. His eyes filled. He sat in the back of the transport with his weakened legs and his thinned arms, his heart at fifty-two beats per minute and wept. The weeping was silent. The guards did not notice. Someone beyond the gate was arguing about cricket.

Bayonne. Southwest France. A camp on a former polo field, the turf still visible beneath the mud, the goal markers repurposed as laundry posts. The camp was fetid. The latrines overflowed. The barracks were overcrowded. The food was inadequate and the water was suspect and the medical facilities were nonexistent.

By regulation, the most senior soldier in the camp, the only officer with a British commission. He weighed perhaps nine stone. His pulse was slow and irregular, the irregularity was a concern he monitored every morning by pressing two fingers to his radial artery and counting for sixty seconds.

A week at Bayonne. During that week he ate, carefully, small portions, the gut still wary, and he observed. He observed the wire, the guards, the routines, the gaps. And he thought about the Pyrenees, which were close, close enough to see on clear days, the mountains rising to the south like a promise in stone.

Then the Germans loaded a group of prisoners onto a train heading north.

II

He found the two sappers in the carriage.

They were young, twenty, perhaps twenty-one, Madrasi, dark-skinned and slight, with the watchful eyes of men who had survived the desert war by paying attention. They had been captured at Gazala. He could see it, the intact quality, the spring still in the body, the readiness.

"The window," he said. In Hindi, because Hindi was what they shared. "Can it be opened?"

Iron bars, set into the wooden frame. But the frame was old, wartime rolling stock, poorly maintained, and the wood around the bars was soft, the screws loose in their holes.

"We can lever them," the taller sapper said. His name was not recorded. History did not preserve it.

A fellow officer, an Indian captain, older, cautious, leaned across the aisle.

"You are mad." "Possibly." "The train is moving. It is moving fast." "Yes." "Possibly mad," the captain said. "Probably dead." "Possibly." The sappers worked the bars in the rhythm of the train's movement so that the sound of iron on wood was covered by the sound of wheels on track. One bar. Two. The third resisted. The taller sapper braced his foot against the wall, pulled. The bar came free. The opening was wide enough for a body. A thin body. A body that had recently lost two stone.

Near Angoulême the train slowed on a curve. The countryside was dark: fields, hedgerows. He calculated: twenty miles per hour, possibly more. The mathematics of impact, deceleration, angle, surface hardness, ran through his mind with the automatic precision of a surgeon computing dosage. Survivable. Probably.

"Now," he said. First out, the taller sapper. A shape dropping through the window, a thud, then nothing. The shorter sapper followed.

He went last. The window frame scraped his ribs and then the air, the cold rush, the ground rising to meet him. He hit the embankment at an angle. The impact was distributed, shoulder, hip, thigh, but his left hand struck a rail tie and the fourth metacarpal snapped with a sharp clean pain that was different from every other pain because this pain was chosen. He had broken his own finger by choosing to be free.

In the grass he lay. The train continued, the sound diminishing, the dark closing over. His finger throbbed. The pain was precise and local, a clean fracture, fourth metacarpal, no displacement, six weeks in a splint. He could set it himself.

The sappers found him. They gathered in the dark, three shapes, breathing hard, checking limbs. They stood in a field near Angoulême and they were free and the freedom was so strange that for several seconds none of them moved.

Then they moved. South. Toward the Pyrenees.

III

They walked for days. Instead of the courtyard's twenty-seven metres, the country opened in every direction. His broken finger he had splinted with a stick and a strip torn from his shirt, the fracture immobilised, the pain manageable.

They walked at night. By day they hid. French peasants helped them. A farmer near Périgueux gave them bread and cheese and pointed south. A woman in a village gave them water from a well and told them to avoid the main roads and the rich people.

In a small village near Toulouse, he made an error. He approached an old Frenchman sitting on a wall and asked the whereabouts of a bridge across the Garonne.

The old man listened. The old man nodded. The old man led them to a police station.

The sappers ran. He did not run. He stood in the doorway and the police looked at him.

They arrested him. They handed him to the Germans. The Germans handed him to the Gestapo.

IV

His first contact with the Gestapo was anything but pleasant.

He would use these words later: measured, understated, the doctor's habit of clinical description applied to his own beating.

Agen first. A cell in the local jail. Small, stone. Two men in leather coats. Not Wehrmacht. The body knew before the mind, the contraction in the abdomen, the adrenal response.

Questions. About the escape. About who had helped. The farmer near Périgueux, they had a name. The woman at the well, they had a village.

He did not speak the names. Then the second man struck. The blow came from the side, open hand, the heel of the palm connecting with his left ear. The sound was enormous, filling the skull, followed by a ringing that was high and continuous. The second blow was to the other side and the third was a fist to the sternum, for three seconds he could not breathe and in those three seconds the room became clear, the bulb, the stains, the scratch marks on the desk's edge where hands had gripped.

They hit him for what he estimated was fifteen minutes. He estimated because the estimating was the doctor's reflex, observe, time, record, and the reflex was all he had. They did not break bones. The blows were to soft tissue: kidneys, abdomen, the muscles of the thighs, and the precision was professional. These were men who knew anatomy from practice.

He did not give them the names. They transferred him first to the cells at Agen. Brutal. The same questions. No answers. Then to Gestapo headquarters at Toulouse. A different technique — more sustained, less precise, administered by a larger man whose patience was thinner.

After one particularly savage thrashing his nose bled for an hour. He timed it. One hour. The blood ran from both nostrils. He let it run because the alternative was to tilt the head, apply pressure, and the applying would have been a cooperation with the body's distress, and he was not cooperating. He sat in the chair and bled.

They knew about Berlin. They knew about Bose. "We'll give you one more chance to join us." He looked at the man. The man was smoking. The cigarette smoke mixed with the smell of blood, his blood, on his shirt, on the floor, tobacco and iron.

"I'm not doing anything of the sort." They beat him again. When it was finished he sat in the chair and breathed. Each breath was a negotiation between the ribs, bruised, possibly cracked, the intercostal muscles in spasm, and the lungs, which required the ribs to move, which required the pain to be overridden.

He breathed. The pain was overridden. The taste in his mouth was iron, the precise ferrous quality of blood, not fresh blood but blood oxidising, old blood, the taste of the inside of the body expressing itself without the body's permission, a chemistry older than medicine.

They sent him back to a cell. The cell was dark and the dark was a relief because in the dark the body could attend to itself, the ribs, the kidneys, the broken finger still in its makeshift splint, the nose whose cartilage felt wrong, shifted, a deviation he could palpate with his uninjured hand.

He lay on the cell floor. The stone was cold and the cold was therapeutic, a crude anti-inflammatory, the body's oldest medicine.

He thought, *I am still alive. The names are still unspoken. The oath still holds.*

V

On April seventeenth they transferred him to Frontstalag 153 at Chartres.

He rode in the back of a truck, bruised ribs and broken finger, shifted nose and the ringing in his left ear. The ear's ringing would not fully subside for weeks. The countryside passed. France in spring. The fields green, the trees budding.

He arrived at Chartres in the late afternoon. The gate opened. And the sound again, as at Bayonne: Indian voices, hundreds of them, the languages overlapping.

I had joined my compatriots. I had reason to be pleased. He was pleased because the camp had Indians and the Indians meant escape, escape meant freedom and freedom meant — he did not finish the sentence. The sentence finished itself underground.

I was determined to get away, come what may.

THE COMPOUND

Chapter 19

I

Frontstalag 153 was a fort, not a castle. Low stone buildings arranged around a central compound. The architecture was military but recent, nineteenth century, Napoleonic, and the walls were thick but not medieval-thick, and the wire was high but not castle-high.

Two thousand five hundred men crowded into corridors built for a fraction of their number. Hindus, Sikhs, Muslims, Christians. Captured in North Africa, mostly, Rommel's desert war had swept up entire Indian divisions and deposited them in camps across occupied Europe.

A bunk in a room with eleven other men. The room smelled different from Colditz. Not stone and damp and boot polish. This room smelled of hair oil and dal, sweat and something floral: incense, perhaps, or the residue of sandalwood soap someone had received in a Red Cross parcel. The smell entered him, a homecoming the body performed without consulting the mind.

Looks. An officer, they could see the insignia. A doctor, word travelled fast. A man who had been at Colditz — faster. Who had met Bose, fastest of all.

The room was warm. The heat arrived from somewhere, a stove burning coal or wood, and the heat was different from the castle's heat, which was absence pretending to be presence. This heat was actual. It pressed against the skin and the skin responded. The body began to sweat in the armpits, at the base of the spine, the sweat the body's recognition that it was no longer in the fortress.

"Is it true?" A Sikh sergeant, turbaned, bearded. "You met Netaji?"

"I met him." "And?" No answer. The sergeant nodded.

II

Slowly, the recovery. Each system restarting at its own pace, the gut learning to digest, the muscles rebuilding fibre by fibre, the ribs knitting where the Gestapo's fists had cracked them, the broken finger setting in its makeshift splint. He ate carefully. The cookhouse served dal and rice and chapati. The first chapati he tore, the bread yielding between his fingers, pliant and warm. He dipped it into dal whose surface shimmered with turmeric and cumin, and the taste that entered his mouth was a place.

On the third day a sepoy came to him with a wound on his forearm, a laceration, shallow, the edges clean. Mazumdar sat the man on a bench and cleaned the wound, dressed it and his hands performed the motions they had not performed in two years. The sepoy thanked him in Hindi and the thanking was ordinary and the ordinariness was the gift, a man who needed a doctor, a doctor who could help, the transaction completed in a language they shared, without the look.

The path from the barracks to the cookhouse was dirt. It was packed hard from the repeated footsteps of men walking to food. He walked it in the evening with Singh, the two of them moving with the queue, the queue moving slowly, the waiting, always the waiting, before the door opened and they stepped into the heat of the preparation, the smell of dal boiling and roti being flattened on hot metal. The waiting had a shape. The shape was familiar. The shape was India.

Through the compound he walked, studying the wire. Three layers. Barbed. Posts at ten-metre intervals. A searchlight tower at each corner. A gate, eighteen feet high, metal, padlocked at night.

He also had rows with the camp commander. Almost every day. The conditions, the food, the sanitation, the medical provision. The rows were strategic and genuine both. The conditions were appalling. He was a doctor and a doctor does not walk past suffering without naming it.

III

Within days, he made his first attempt.

The window in the eastern barracks had bars. Iron, set into wooden frames. The frames were old, the wood softened by a hundred winters. He worked at night with a blade stolen from the cookhouse, sawing through the wood with the patience of a surgeon debriding a wound. Two nights. The bars loosened.

On the third night he removed them. The bars came free with a sound like a sigh and the window opened to the dark.

The outer wall was twenty feet high. Along the top, broken glass set in cement. He had prepared, a folded blanket over his shoulder. He crossed the yard. The searchlight was on the far arc, eleven seconds, and in those eleven seconds he reached the wall and began to climb.

The stone was old and the mortar had eroded and the handholds were adequate. He reached the top. He laid the blanket. He swung one leg over and for a moment, no more than two seconds, he was straddling the wall, the camp behind him, France in front of him, the night air cool on his face. The floodlight found him.

White, total — a fixed light from the guardhouse roof that someone had switched on. He was a brown man on a white wall in a white beam.

He did not jump. The machine gun was already tracking. He could hear it, the barrel swivelling in its mount, and the probability of being hit before he reached cover was high. He raised his hands.

IV

Six weeks in solitary. Stone walls. A door. A slot for food. A bucket.

In solitary, a doctor's self-examination. Pulse: morning and evening, two fingers on the radial artery, sixty seconds. Cognitive function: he recited the bones of the hand: scaphoid, lunate, triquetral, pisiform, trapezium, trapezoid, capitate, hamate, and when the hand was finished he did the foot, and when the foot was finished he did the cranial nerves, and the reciting was survival, the mind keeping itself alive by walking the corridors of knowledge the way the body had once walked the courtyard at Colditz.

Six weeks. Then the door opened and the light was enormous and the compound was loud with the sound of Indian men.

V

After solitary they gave him a guard.

The guard was Algerian. Young, bored, armed with a rifle he carried with indifference. He followed Mazumdar everywhere. To the cookhouse. To the infirmary. To the latrines. *He made my life unbearable and followed me everywhere I went, even to the WC.*

At night the guard went off duty to wherever guards went when they were not watching the prisoners. They locked him with a handful of other troublemakers, men who had attempted escape, who had refused orders, men for whom the rules had changed the moment they violated them. One half of a three-storey block, the windows barred, the door bolted with heavy iron, five Algerian guards with machine guns on the floor below.

Sikhs, mostly — big men, cavalry, infantry. They slept on the floor. They talked at night in Punjabi and Hindi and the talk was always about the same thing, the wire, the wall, the guards, the gap.

Among them was a giant.

VI

Dariao Singh. Sowar, Second Royal Lancers, Gardner's Horse. A Jat Sikh from the Punjab.

He was well over six feet tall. His beard was flowing, dark, maintained with the discipline of a man for whom the beard was covenant. His turban was dark blue, the colour of his regiment, wound with precision even here.

His hands were the size of soup plates. Enormous hands — broad across the palm, the fingers thick and long. They were hands that had spent a life with horses, the grip formed by reins and lances. They rested on his knees when he sat, patient, with the patience of a horseman.

He spoke little. When he spoke, the words were Punjabi-accented English, clipped, military.

"You are the doctor who climbed the wall." "I am the doctor who was caught on the wall." "Next time, don't use the wall." Mazumdar looked at him, at the giant frame, the steady hands, the eyes that were calculating even when the mouth was still. Singh was not making conversation. He was making an offer.

"You've been thinking about it." "Since I arrived." "Why haven't you gone?" "I had no one to go with."

They sat in the troublemakers' block with the machine guns below and the barred windows above and the night pressing against the glass.

"Eleven seconds," Singh said. "You've timed the searchlight." "Eleven seconds is enough." They sat. The searchlight swept beyond the barred window. Eleven seconds of dark, then the light, then eleven seconds again.

"Enough," Mazumdar said. "If the rest is right." "Then we make the rest right." Singh's hands rested on his knees. The hands the size of soup plates. Still. Waiting.

THE WALL

Chapter 20

I-A

The barracks were silent at night but not truly silent. Beneath silence were layers, the small percussion of settling wood, the distant machinery of the camp's generator, the breathing of thirty men on thirty narrow bunks. Mazumdar could distinguish them all by the third week in the troublemakers' block. Each man's respiration was a signature: rapid, shallow, laboured, calm. He had noted them as he noted symptoms in a ward, the consumption case in bunk seven, the man with cardiac arrhythmia in bunk two. Observation without intervention. The doctor's habit persists even when medicine is forbidden.

Singh's breathing was different. Low, voluminous, the rhythm of a man whose lungs had developed on the central plain where there was nothing to stop the wind. The diaphragm moving with a large and ordinary efficiency. Mazumdar could hear it now from the adjacent bunk, Singh on his back, awake but still. The man did not speak. He had said nothing for an hour. In the darkness it was almost companionable, the presence of someone who did not require words.

The moonlight came through the barred window in stripes. Four bars, four pale lines across the floor boards and the lower bunks, moving fractionally westward as the moon descended. Mazumdar was watching them move. The slight shift every few minutes, unmeasurable at the moment but visible across an hour. Everything moved. Even stones moved. The moon moved. The stars moved. The bars stayed still. That was the only true thing in this room.

Singh's hand was resting on his thigh. The hand was very large, the palm broad, the fingers square-tipped from years of reins. The skin was marked with small scars. Mazumdar had observed these hands working. They had a particular quality: no wasted motion, no visible deliberation. The hand would move to accomplish something and it would accomplish it. There was no struggle in between. His own hands were different, his surgeon's hands, precise but questioning. Always asking the body for permission. Singh's hands did not ask.

Somewhere in the main compound, voices. Indian voices, several men speaking together, the acoustics of the night air carrying the sound up and across the fence. Tamil, perhaps. Or Telugu. The words were indistinct but the fact of them was electric. Mazumdar had not heard an Indian voice in months. The sound was physical, a hand on the arm, and he found himself tracking it until it dissolved into the ambient noise of the camp.

"The Phalgu sounds like that." He had said it without intention. The words arrived already voiced.

Singh turned his head. The bars cast lines across his face. "In the flood season. When the water was above ground. The sound of it in the dark. Many voices." Mazumdar stopped. The description had been precise and it had been unnecessary.

Singh did not require explanation. But some part of him, some part that was not the man who had learned to survive in camps, had needed to speak it aloud.

Singh lay still for a moment. Then, "The plains before dawn. Not water. Horses. The whole command moving, you hear it before you see it. The ground carried the sound."

It was more than Singh usually offered. Mazumdar registered this. The man was permitting reciprocity. Mazumdar's memory of water allowed Singh to offer his own memory back. The exchange was in Hindi, a language neither had spoken since arrival in France, and the shift was so complete it was as if they had stepped into a different room. The room remained the same. The bars remained. But the air had changed.

They lay in silence after that. The moonlight continued its minute westward journey. Somewhere below, on the floor of the ground level where the guard post was, a cough. A man clearing his throat. The sound carried up through the stone. The guard was awake. The attention of the guard was a weight in the room.

But Singh's breathing did not change. The large diaphragm continued its even descent and rise. The man beside him was not anxious. Anxiety would have registered as a change in rhythm, a quickening, a tightness in the exhalation. There was none of that. Singh was breathing the way a man breathes when the thing he is preparing for is already done, already decided, and the only remaining task is to be still.

Mazumdar understood this on the second night in the troublemakers' block. The understanding did not come as revelation. It came as silence, as the sound of another man's breathing, as the moonlight moving by imperceptible degrees across the floorboards. Singh had been planning for months. Singh was still. The difference between those two facts was the knowledge that Singh had already succeeded.

I

Singh had been planning for months. This was what Mazumdar understood on the second night in the troublemakers' block, when Singh began to describe the compound as a cavalry officer describes terrain before a charge, every sightline mapped, every guard rotation timed, every weakness identified and filed. What he had lacked was a partner.

Now he had one. They worked fast. The wall was two feet thick. Stone, not brick, old French military construction, designed to withstand cannon shot. Singh had found the weak point, a storeroom beneath the eastern barracks where the mortar had degraded, where moisture had softened the joints. He had been working on it alone, night after night, with a stolen mess knife. The debris carried out in pockets and scattered across the compound at dawn.

Singh showed him the progress. Three sections where the mortar had already failed, where the stone could be pulled rather than cut. The wall was nearly through.

Singh did the remaining work in two nights. The chipping had a sound. A small, regular, mineral percussion, stone on stone, the mortar giving way in grains, and the sound, in the dark storeroom at two in the morning, recalled another sound, the pestle in his mother's kitchen, grinding spices.

Mortar and mortar. The word was the same word.

II

The window was the next obstacle. A ground-floor window on the eastern face, nailed shut and sealed with two thick sheets of tin. Singh produced a blade smuggled into the camp inside a Red Cross cricket bat. The tin resisted. But Singh's hands, the hands the size of soup plates, the horseman's grip, the thenar eminence overdeveloped from years of reins, worked the blade beneath the tin's edge and levered, slow, and the tin bent and the nails loosened one by one, the sound of each loosening absorbed by Singh's palm pressed flat against the metal.

"Where did you get the blade?" "A Sikh always has a blade, Doctor." Singh's humour was dry and rare and delivered without expression. Mazumdar found himself smiling. The smiling was unfamiliar, involuntary. Singh surprised him. The man's competence was a kind of joy.

They cut two bars. They left the cuts concealed with a paste of stone dust and water, the bars resting in their housings, removable in seconds. The window became a door. The door led to the open ground. The open ground led to the wire.

III

The wire required tools. Heavy pliers, stolen from the maintenance shed in a sequence of thefts so incremental that no single absence registered. A handle here, a jaw there, the parts assembled over weeks and hidden in a space behind a loose board that Singh had found.

They practised the crawl. At night, in the barracks corridor, on their elbows and knees, timing each other, ten yards in eleven seconds. Then ten. Then nine. The margin was the difference between the searchlight's passage and its return.

Singh was better at it. Low to the ground, the hips moving with a fluidity the surgeon's body could not match. Mazumdar compensated with precision, placing each elbow, each knee, deliberately.

"You crawl like a doctor," Singh said. "Meaning?" "Carefully. Too carefully. The ground won't break." "The ground isn't what concerns me." "Then what?" "The sound. My bag." The medical bag. The bag's buckle struck the ground with each forward motion.

Singh took the bag. He shortened the strap. He padded the buckle with a strip of cloth torn from a blanket. He returned it without comment.

IV

June third. The night was warm and the sky was clouded, no moon, no stars. The searchlight's beam would find less in cloud-dark than in clear-dark.

They waited until two in the morning. The guard change, a ten-minute window when the new shift was settling in. Ten minutes of reduced vigilance added to eleven seconds of darkness between searchlight sweeps.

Singh peeled back the tin. The sheets came away from the frame without sound. The window opened to the night. Cool air. The smell of grass and earth and a bakery, somewhere distant, the town of Chartres beginning its pre-dawn work.

They went through the wall first. The stone section Singh had loosened came apart in his hands like bread, the pieces stacked neatly in the storeroom, the gap just wide enough for a man's shoulders. Through the wall, through the window, into the dark.

The ground was wet. He could feel it immediately, the dew on the grass, the cold spreading through his shirt as he lowered himself to his elbows. Singh was beside him. The searchlight was mid-arc, moving away.

Eleven seconds. They began to crawl.

THE WIRE

Chapter 21

They went flat. The open ground between the building and the perimeter of Frontstalag 153 was five hundred yards of grass and bare earth, sloping gently toward the wire. The searchlight was already moving, a white arm sweeping from the tower at the northwest corner, describing an arc that took eleven seconds to complete. He had timed it from inside. Eleven seconds of dark, then the light, then eleven seconds again. In those intervals they moved. Elbows and knees. The crawl they had practised in the compound at night when the guards were playing cards, dragging themselves along the barracks wall until Singh was satisfied that Mazumdar could cover ten yards in the time between sweeps.

The grass was wet. He could feel it through his shirt, the cold spreading across his chest and stomach, and the mud beneath the grass had a particular sucking quality that gripped his elbows each time he planted them. His medical bag hung from his neck on a strap he had shortened twice and it swung with each movement, bumping his sternum, the buckle made a small sound against the ground each time his chest dipped and he could not stop it and could not unhear it.

Eleven seconds. They moved. The light passed over them and the grass turned white and they pressed into earth. His face in the mud. The taste of it, sharp and mineral and iron and faecal. Then dark and they moved.

The first hundred yards went quickly. His arms were fresh and the mud was shallow and the intervals felt long enough, eleven seconds in which a man could cover a surprising amount of ground if the alternative to covering ground was the alternative. But at a hundred yards the slope changed. The earth became softer, wetter, and his elbows sank deeper with each plant, and the suction when he pulled them free made a sound his fear magnified into a report audible at the tower, at the guardhouse, in Berlin. He pressed lower. His chin ploughed a furrow. Singh, ahead, was a dark shape that moved and stopped, moved and stopped. Mazumdar fixed on the shape and followed it the way you follow a light in fog.

At two hundred yards his shoulders began to report. A burning across both trapezii, sustained load, prone position, predictable onset. His hip flexors followed. Then his fingers, which had gone intermittently numb from dragging his weight across cold ground. He flexed them between intervals, one hand at a time, opening and closing the fist in the mud while the searchlight passed.

At three hundred yards the arithmetic failed. He had been counting intervals, a discipline that gave the crawl structure, each eleven-second sweep a unit of progress, but the counting stopped around the twenty-eighth or thirtieth sweep and what replaced it was a state. The state of crawling. The mud and the grass and the light and the dark and the body working and the mind no longer supervising the work but simply inhabiting it, as you inhabit a fever, not directing it, not resisting it, enduring it.

Then the body alone, the elbows and knees moving in rhythm, the chest dragging, the medical bag swinging with each heave forward. No interval. No counting. Only the mud, the grass, the pulling. The darkness pressing down. The body doing what the body does when the mind steps away. The arms burned. The fingers had gone numb. His face was in the earth and the earth was in his mouth, the earth and the mouth were the same thing now. Move. Pull. Forward.

The five hundred yards took an hour and forty minutes. He was aware of time passing the way you are aware of an infusion drip, not by the drops but by the level in the bag. The level was dropping. They had perhaps four hours of full dark remaining and the wire was still ahead.

A sound ahead. Singh, stopped. Mazumdar pulled himself alongside and the wire was there. It materialised in pieces, a post first, then the horizontal lines between the posts, then the barbs catching what little light the sky offered. The first fence. Three feet high, seven horizontal strands fixed to concrete posts. Standard military issue, the same galvanised twist, the barbs spaced at four-inch intervals, designed to slow it into the range of accurate fire.

Singh already had the cutters out. Two pieces of metal bedpost, sharpened and bent into jaws over eleven nights. They were not good cutters. They were what could be made by a man with strong hands and a piece of iron and no tools except the cell floor. Singh gripped the first strand near the base and squeezed. The muscles in his forearm stood out under the skin like cables, and the wire resisted and then the strand parted with a sound like a fingernail being clipped.

He watched Singh's hands. They moved in quarter-inches. Easing the jaws around each wire. Waiting for the steel to give. Those hands could pull a man over a wall by the collar. Tonight they moved as if the wire were a suture and the dark a wound that must be closed from inside.

In Gaya his father's hands had moved with that quality. Different hands, different work, but the same thing beneath the competence, something he could see but not name. In the surgery in Gaya the kerosene light had turned everything amber and his father's wrists had turned inside a patient with an authority that came from somewhere the Royal College had never mapped. There had been a moment before each incision when those hands rested on the body. Not pressing. Not examining. Resting. The way you rest your hand on a wall to know if the building is sound. The patient would go still. Then the cut. And it was precise. And in his second year at the Royal College he had tried to replicate that pause, hand on chest, wait, then cut, and the registrar had looked at him and said nothing and the nothing had been enough and he had not done it again.

The searchlight swept. He pressed flat. Mud in his mouth. The light passed. Singh's hand was already on the next strand.

Seven strands. The first took nine minutes. He counted that one. The remaining six were faster. Singh finding the technique, the jaws of the cutter learning the wire's resistance, the rhythm establishing itself. Singh cut the bottom two completely and bent the third upward and they pushed through on their stomachs, the wire pressing against their backs. A barb caught Mazumdar's shirt between the shoulder blades. He felt it bite the skin beneath. He lay still while Singh reached back and freed the fabric with two fingers, the gesture precise and impersonal.

Between the first fence and the second they lay flat. The ground here was different: harder, drier, a strip of packed earth between the fence lines. The searchlight came and Mazumdar closed his eyes because the light on the inside of his eyelids was preferable to the light on the wire.

His heart rate was elevated. He could feel it in his throat without touching his pulse. A hundred. More. Not a rhythm to be concerned about, just fear, fear borrowing the body's infrastructure to announce itself, and the clinical mind filing the announcement under the wrong heading because the correct heading was not in the clinical vocabulary.

Shaking hands, not from cold. There was a grasshopper in the grass near his face. He could see its legs. It did not move.

The searchlight passed. He lay in the dark between the fences and listened. Wind in the grass. Singh breathing. The distant mechanical hum of a generator or the searchlight's motor turning on its axis. The camp behind them was a dark mass against a dark sky. No alarm. No shout. No dog. Only the light, sweeping its arc, finding nothing where two men lay in the dirt between the wire.

Singh touched his arm. They moved. The second fence. Four lines of wire strung between lower posts, more widely spaced. Faster. The sound (a small precise *tick* each time a strand parted) seemed to Mazumdar the loudest sound in occupied France, audible certainly at the tower and probably at the guardhouse and possibly in Chartres itself, though he understood that this was the fear again, borrowing the acoustics of the imagination because the actual sound was quieter than the grasshopper's breathing, if grasshoppers breathed, which they did, through spiracles, ten pairs, arranged segmentally along the —

He stopped himself. A man lying in mud cataloguing insect respiration was a man whose mind had lost its purchase on the relevant.

They cleared the second fence. The ground between the second fence and the perimeter smelled different, less mud, more grass, the camp receding behind them like a breath being released. A third line of wire, single strand, knee height. Singh reached for it with the cutters. The strand snapped before the jaws closed, rusted through, the tension stored in the wire releasing all at once, and the loose end whipped back and struck the concrete post with a sound like a pistol shot. They pressed flat. The searchlight was mid-arc. It swept toward them and the wire on the ground caught the light, shone and the post stood in the beam like a man standing at attention and the light moved past and found nothing that moved and the dark returned. Mazumdar's face was in the dirt. His heart was in his ears. The loose wire had struck his forearm and left a line of heat, superficial, no debridement required, and the diagnosis arrived before he had decided whether it hurt.

They did not move. One full sweep. Two. On the third dark interval Singh reached back and pulled the loose wire aside and they crawled through.

Somewhere beyond the wire a dog barked once and stopped.

The gate. It rose out of the dark as the castle had risen out of the dark more than a year ago: suddenly, completely, a thing that had been theoretical becoming iron. Eighteen feet. The vertical bars were spaced six inches apart. At the top, three coils of barbed wire bolted to a crossbar, the wire kinked and rusted and ugly against the sky.

Singh stood. The act of standing after three hours prone was itself a violence: rising into the vertical, into visibility, into the space where the searchlight could find him. He did not pause. He gripped the bars and went up.

He climbed as Mazumdar had seen him go through a wall, as if the obstacle were a temporary misunderstanding between his body and the architecture. His feet found the crossbars. His hands moved upward in a rhythm that was continuous. At eight feet a bar was wet and his boot slipped, his weight swung and Mazumdar heard the gate take the impact, a deep iron sound, a vibration that travelled down the bars into the ground. Singh hung by his arms. His boots found purchase. He continued.

At twelve feet the bars narrowed. The searchlight was coming. Singh pressed himself against the gate and the light swept the ground below, the lower bars threw shadows and Singh was above the beam, folded against the iron, his body a dark shape against the dark sky. The light passed. Singh climbed. At the top, the wire. The cutters worked blind, by feel, Singh's hands finding the strands among the coils and placing the jaws and squeezing. Three snips. The wire peeled back from the crossbar like skin from a wound.

He waited at the top. The searchlight came again. He pressed flat against the crossbar and the light swept below, found nothing and the dark returned.

Then the hand came down. Enormous. The fingers spread wide.

Mazumdar gripped the lowest bar. His arms took his weight with a reluctance he felt in both shoulders simultaneously. He climbed. His feet slipped on the second bar. He hung. His medical bag swung out from his body. For a moment he was attached to the gate by his fingers and nothing else and his fingers were not optimistic. He found the bar with his right foot. He climbed. The searchlight swept below him, the bars throwing shadows that rotated as the beam passed, and he pressed flat against the iron and waited. Dark. He climbed. It would not have survived peer review.

At eight feet his arms burned. At twelve his grip was failing, the fingers opening involuntarily, the flexors in his forearms trembling, and he thought with absolute clarity, I cannot do this. And the thought was calm and clinical and wrong. He gripped tighter. He found the next bar. He climbed.

Singh's hand closed around his wrist and pulled. The strength of the pull hauled him upward. His feet scrabbled, his ribs hit the crossbar. The remaining wire bit into his forearm in two places, both superficial, both irrelevant, and then he was at the top and the countryside opened beneath them.

Fields. A road running east. A darker line that might be a hedgerow or might be a ditch. France, occupied and asleep, enormous and dark. The smell of it — not the camp smell, not wire and mud, latrine, but grass and earth and distance, the smell of a country that went on for nine hundred kilometres in the direction they needed to go.

Singh dropped to the other side. Quiet. A cavalryman who knew how to land.

Mazumdar dropped. His ankle turned on a stone. It held. He stood.

Singh was beside him. In the dark he was tall and his breathing was steady, his hand found Mazumdar's hand and held it — not to pull but to steady, the grip firm and brief, firm and brief, he had done something and wanted Mazumdar to know it was done and they were here and the wire was behind them.

"*Shabash, Doctor Sahib.*" Said quietly. Two words in Hindi in a field in France in the middle of a war, in the dark, on the far side of the wire, by a man whose name would disappear from the record as completely as the river at Gaya disappears into the ground. Said to a man who had not heard the word in three years.

Neither of them moved. Three seconds. The searchlight swept the empty ground on the other side of the gate. It found nothing.

Singh threw the cutters into the pond beyond the fence. Then they ran. They ran for an hour without stopping. Two men, one short, thick-waisted, carrying a leather bag that slapped against his hip with every stride; the other a head taller, bearded, his legs covering ground at a pace the shorter man could match only by running where the taller man loped. Their boots on the wet earth. The rain on their faces. The dark ahead and the camp behind and the distance between the two growing with every stride. The running was not graceful. It was not the running of athletes or soldiers on parade. It was the running of men whose bodies had been confined for years and were now unconfined and the unconfining released a thing that was not adrenaline and not fear but older, the animal knowledge that the body is made for this, for the open ground, for the dark, for the running, and the confinement was the aberration and the running was the correction.

His medical bag slapped against his hip. His lungs burned. His legs, the surgeon's legs, the legs that had crawled five hundred yards on elbows and knees, found a rhythm in the mud and the rhythm was Singh's rhythm and they ran together, the two bodies synchronised by urgency and by a thing neither would name: joy. The running was joy. The rain was joy. The mud and the burning lungs and the dark and the distance were joy.

After an hour they slowed. They walked. The walking was the beginning of a different journey.

THE WALK

Chapter 22

I

They walked south.

The first night was speed, distance from the camp, distance from the dogs, distance from the searchlights that would not notice their absence until morning roll call. They walked through fields, through hedgerows, through the edges of a France that was occupied and dark. The moon was behind cloud. The stars were behind cloud. The ground was beneath their feet and the ground held.

By dawn they had covered twenty kilometres, maybe more, the distance accumulating in their legs. They found a wood: small, dense, impenetrable to casual observation, the undergrowth thick enough to hide two men effectively, and they lay in the undergrowth and listened instead to the sounds of the occupied forest around them.

"We walk at night," Singh said. "We hide by day." "For how long?" "Six hundred miles."

The first week established the rhythm. Night: walk. South and east, toward Switzerland. Using the stars when the clouds allowed, the roads when the roads were empty, the fields when the roads were not. They avoided villages. They avoided checkpoints. They avoided everything that contained people because people contained eyes.

Day: hide. Woods, barns, ditches. Once a church: empty, unlocked, the stone cool and the silence holy in a way that had nothing to do with religion. They slept in shifts. Two hours, then switch. Shallow sleep, full of sounds: waking instant, the eyes open before the mind, the hands already moving.

They ate what they found. Apples from an orchard, the skin taut and cool against his teeth, the flesh mealy with late season. Turnips from a field, pulled from the earth still gritty with soil. Water from streams, cupped in hands that were cracked and dirty, the water so cold it ached in the back of the throat. Singh knew how to forage, the cavalry training, the months in North Africa. Mazumdar's medical knowledge kept them alive differently: he monitored their feet, their hydration, the early signs of infection. He treated Singh's blisters with strips torn from his shirt. He checked their pulses each morning, the ritual that kept the doctor in him alive when everything else was animal.

II

The second week they were nearly caught.

A checkpoint on a road they had not seen until they were on it, a barrier, two soldiers, a lantern. The cigarettes' glow was the warning. Singh pulled Mazumdar into a ditch and they lay in the water: cold, silted, the water reaching their chests, while the soldiers finished their cigarettes twenty feet away. The conversation was German. Something about leave. Something about a girl. The soldiers laughed. Young men at war who were not at this moment thinking about war.

They crossed fields after that. No more roads. The fields were slower but safer and the safety was worth the blisters, the brambles and the barbed-wire fences that had to be navigated in darkness by feel, the wire finding them before they found it.

A French farmer helped them in the third week. They had been spotted, inevitable, two brown men could not walk six hundred miles through occupied France without being seen by someone, and the farmer had seen them from his kitchen window and had come out with bread and cheese and a bottle of wine and had said nothing at all. He had placed the food carefully on the wall of his barn and turned and gone back inside without looking back.

They ate the bread. The cheese was sharp and strong. Outside a large house in the fourth week, desperate, Mazumdar knocked on the door. The woman who answered was well-dressed, the house behind her warm and lit, smelling of roast lamb and rosemary. She looked at them, two brown men, filthy, one in the remnants of a military uniform, the other enormous and bearded. The Comtesse d'Impley slammed the door. Through the wood she shouted that she would call the gendarmerie. They left.

They crossed three rivers. The first two were shallow enough to wade. The Saône was different. The bridge was guarded, a single soldier, the rifle on his shoulder, and they lay in the reeds for an hour before crossing upstream, in the dark, the water to their waists, the current pulling at them. Singh held the medical bag above his head. Mazumdar held Singh's arm. They emerged on the far bank, soaked, shaking, alive.

Near Dôle, in the sixth week, an elderly woman opened her door before they knocked. She brought them inside. She fed them bread, cheese, wine. She said little, her French accented with a quality Mazumdar could not place, the accent of a life lived entirely within the radius of this house and this garden.

She sent her grandson, a boy of twelve, to guide them through the woods to the next valley. The boy walked ahead of them without speaking, his bare feet on the path, the path invisible to them but visible to him because the path was his. At the edge of the woods the boy pointed south. Then he turned and walked back.

They never learned her name.

III

One night, a barn outside Bourges, Singh slept first. Mazumdar lay awake and watched him. The hands that had climbed the gate were curled loosely on the straw, the fingers open, the grip released. Singh's face in sleep was different — the jaw unclenched, the mouth slightly open, the breathing deep and unhurried, the face of a man who is simply asleep. He muttered something. Punjabi, perhaps. A name, or a word for home. His hand reached across the straw toward a warmth that was not there. Then the hand settled. The breathing continued.

The weeks compressed. Walking became the medium of their existence, the body in motion, the feet on ground, the ground changing beneath them as France changed from flat to hilly to mountainous. The Jura appeared on the horizon in the sixth week, a line of blue that could have been cloud but was not, that was solid, that was Switzerland's western wall.

Singh weakened in the sixth week. A fever — low-grade, persistent. Mazumdar monitored it with the instruments available to him, his fingers on Singh's wrist at dawn and dusk, counting the pulse against his own breathing, a field technique from Edinburgh, the body as metronome. The pulse was elevated. Ninety-two at rest. Ninety-eight by midday. The skin warm and dry, the persistent low burn of a body that had walked four hundred miles on turnips and stream water, running out of the reserves it had been consuming since Chartres.

He examined Singh each morning in whatever barn or ditch they occupied. The lymph nodes, submandibular, cervical, axillary, palpated with fingers that were cracked and dirty but still precise, still capable of the distinctions Edinburgh had taught. No significant lymphadenopathy. The lungs clear, he listened with his ear pressed to Singh's back, the ribs prominent, the intercostal spaces visible, the breathing audible without a stethoscope because the chest wall had thinned to a membrane. No crackles. No consolidation. The fever was exhaustion, not infection. The body announcing its limits.

"Keep walking." "I'm walking." "Slower. But walking." Singh walked. He walked with the gait of will arguing with fever, the legs moving because they had been told to move, the stride shortened, the balance maintained by a Sikh cavalryman's training in the saddle, the body's centre of gravity held low, the hips steady. The trust was not Ferguson's trust, Ferguson's had been witness, sitting beside a bunk. Singh's was the trust of motion, of walking beside a man through occupied country because the man had said *walk* and the saying was enough.

At night Mazumdar lay beside Singh in barns and listened to the breathing. Thirty-two respirations per minute. Elevated. The normal adult range was twelve to twenty. He counted the respirations against the dark, *ek, dui, tin, char,* the counting Bengali, involuntary, the numbers arriving from the same place his mother's voice arrived, the base layer that the years had not eroded because numbers were below language, numbers were the body's own arithmetic.

Singh's skin was hot through the cloth. Mazumdar placed his palm flat on Singh's forehead, the gesture not medical, not clinical, the gesture of a man caring for another man in the dark. The forehead was dry. The temperature was high. He estimated 38.5, closer to 39. He had no thermometer. He had his hands.

The fifteen kilometres per day became ten, became eight. Singh's fever broke on day thirty-nine. It broke at dawn, in a barn, the sweat soaking through his shirt and the shirt steaming in the cold morning air. Mazumdar was awake, he had been awake for most of the night, monitoring the breathing, counting the pulse at intervals. The sweat came in a wave. Singh's shirt darkened from the collar down. The breaking was visible, a tide moving through the cloth, the body releasing what it had held. He opened his eyes and the eyes were clear.

"How far?" "Two days. Perhaps three." "Then we walk."

IV

The border was not a line. It was a landscape: hills, dense forest, green pasture. There was no wall, no gate, no visible wire. Just the landscape changing beneath their feet as they climbed.

They crossed at altitude. A ridge: steep, rocky, the footing uncertain and treacherous in the dark. Singh went first, moving with the confidence of a cavalryman on difficult terrain. Mazumdar followed, less confident. The medical bag swung against his hip, the rhythm of six weeks, the weight of six weeks of walking.

Nine o'clock. July thirteenth. They crossed near Malcombe, the border completely unmarked, no signs or barriers, the ridge giving way to a gentler slope, the grass Swiss grass now, the same grass as French grass, identical in every way, but Swiss, and that difference meant everything.

He knew it before they confirmed it. The body knew. The sternum released a tension whose presence he had not registered until the release, the breath arriving deeper, the air thinner but expandable, the ribs consenting to full expansion as they had not consented in six weeks because six weeks the body had been a prisoner and now the body, crossing an unmarked line, understood that the prisoner and the prison were separable, that the body could move from one state to another without the mind announcing the transition.

By midnight they had staggered into the police station at La Rippe. An Indian officer carrying a battered medical bag and a bearded Sikh trooper a foot taller than the policeman who opened the door, both filthy, both skeletal, both grinning. The constable made a telephone call. The telephone call set in motion the machinery of Swiss neutrality.

THE NEUTRAL

Chapter 23

I

Processed with efficiency and without warmth.

A military post. Forms. A doctor, not Mazumdar, a Swiss doctor, a neutral doctor, who examined them with professional interest, cataloguing the effects of an ordeal he had never experienced. Weight, Mazumdar had lost twelve kilos since Colditz. Feet: blistered, infected in three places, the infections controlled but present. Cardiac: regular, rate sixty-eight, no murmur. The doctor recorded these numbers on a form. The form was filed.

They were separated. Singh to one facility, Mazumdar to another. The separation was procedural, nationality, rank, category, and the procedure did not consult their preference. Six weeks of walking, of hiding, and the separation was a form on a desk.

"Singh." Singh turned. He was standing in a corridor, being guided toward a door. The corridor was clean. The door was open, an administration's opening. Between them the corridor stretched, ten or twelve metres, and Singh was walking, Mazumdar was standing and the distance grew.

"Thank you." Singh stopped. He turned fully. The corridor held them. Singh nodded. The same nod he had given on the wall at

Chartres: quiet, professional, containing everything. Then he walked through the door. The door did not close behind him. It stayed open.

They did not see each other again.

II

Weeks of decompression.

Sleep first. Deep, animal sleep, the body collecting a debt three years in the making. The mattress was soft. The sheets were cotton. The pillow was a thing he had forgotten existed. His neck was not accustomed to support; it held tension even in sleep, the muscles expecting stone, resisting the softness. By the third night the neck had begun to capitulate, the shoulders descending from their habitual elevation, the body learning that softness was not a threat.

Bread with a crust that cracked under his teeth, the interior white and soft, so unlike the dense dark German loaves that his jaw didn't know what to do with the softness. Cheese sharp and cool on the tongue. Chocolate melting against the roof of his mouth, flooding the palate with forgotten sweetness. Milk cold from the jug, the fat of it coating his lips. He woke and ate, slept and the cycle repeated, the body's verdict on what had been done to it.

He wrote to his father. The letter was short, written in green ink on blue paper, heavy stock, the colour of a particular sky, the ink vivid against it. He would write this way for the rest of his life. The combination was unmistakable, a letter from Mazumdar announced itself before it was opened. He did not describe the castle or the hunger strike or the walk. He wrote, *I am well. I am in Switzerland. I will come home.* The words were inadequate and the inadequacy was a choice, a choice, certain experiences could not survive the passage from event to language, that the words available to him were not large enough for what had happened, and that the attempt to make them large enough would produce noise.

He did not write about Bose. He did not write about the oath. He did not write about Ferguson or Ellingham or the woman on the train or the Phalgu or the Bengali heard in a Berlin station. These were his. They lived in the place where Bengali lived, beneath the English, underground.

Then the decompression ended and what followed was, by his own account, a good life. Good food. Good wine. He was billeted in Montreux, the lake, the mountains, the particular Swiss light that made everything look clean and orderly, as if the landscape had been administered by the same bureaucracy that administered the forms. The cold arrived in the mornings, the altitude cold, different from the Saxon cold, sharper, present in the clarity of the air rather than in the dampness of stone. The lake was cold when he swam in it in summer, the water shocking the body into attention, the muscle fibres contracting, the breath coming short. The cold was a fact he could measure with his hand, his wrist, the surface of his skin. It was an honest cold, not the dishonest cold of a castle that had learned to retain it. He went back to medicine. Allied servicemen who had escaped to Switzerland needed treatment, frostbite, malnutrition, the various degradations of captivity and flight, and he treated them with the hands that had set a broken finger on a French embankment and dressed blisters in barns and pressed two fingers to his own radial artery every morning for sixteen days. The hands knew what to do. The hands had always known.

A specialist tuberculosis clinic in Locarno. The studying was a restoration, the mind returning to the systematic accumulation of knowledge, the lectures, the case studies, the ordered progression from symptom to diagnosis to treatment. After three years of enforced idleness interrupted by violence, the act of opening a textbook was itself therapeutic, the pages turning beneath his fingers like the pages of a life resuming.

Billiards. Bridge. A naval petty officer named Hammond became his regular partner, a man who laughed easily and played cards with attentive recklessness, he had survived a submarine war and could not be frightened by a bad hand. They played in the British club at Montreux, companionship, the simple pleasure of another man's company organised around a green felt surface and the geometry of angles.

The officers who had served in British India were the worst. They had a term for men like him, *Bengali Baboo*, and the term was a weapon, two words that compressed a century of colonial contempt into a sound. He heard it. He did not always hear who said it. The term travelled through the officer community at Montreux without attribution, without confrontation, a sound in the air, a texture in the looking.

At the British club, he brought Hammond for a game of billiards. A straightforward evening, two men, a table, the click of ivory on ivory. An officer at the door stopped them.

"I'm afraid Hammond is only a petty officer. The snooker table is reserved for commissioned officers."

The regulation existed. The regulation was being applied now, at this moment, to this man. He left. Hammond left with him. Neither man commented on what had happened.

A British colonel accosted Mazumdar outside the club.

"Speak to your countrymen. Tell them not to socialise with Swiss girls."

"Colonel, I shall not do it. As long as British officers socialise with Swiss girls, then I will."

"You're wasting your time," Mazumdar said. "I'm supposed to be free, so don't chain me. You can't chain me."

He met Elianne. ### Montreux: The Lake The afternoon was autumn, the light already the colour of old brass. He was sitting on a stone bench facing the water when she came down the path, along a path lined with yellowing plane trees.

She was carrying a book. "May I sit?" The question was asked in French, and the French was asking permission for the body to take up space on a shared bench. He moved. Four inches. The bench was long. Space remained on both sides.

She sat. She opened the book. Her left hand held the spine; her right turned the pages. The right hand's thumbnail was bitten short, the only imperfection in an otherwise composed surface, and the biting was recent, the skin around the nail pink and tender, the work of the flexor digitorum superficialis visible beneath the skin each time the thumb curled involuntarily toward the finger. She did not notice him noticing. The book was in French — Colette. She did not speak. The lake spoke. Water against stone. The sound was mineral, clean, the mineral sound of water cooled from summer.

He waited for the question. The question that came from every woman he had spoken to in England, from the officers' wives, from the girl at the Red Cross desk, from every pair of eyes that had contained the unvoiced, *But what are you?*

She turned a page. The page had been read before, the spine of the book had been broken and broken again at this exact spot. A favourite passage. Her breathing was even, twelve or thirteen cycles per minute, the respiration of a body at rest, a body that had not been asked to account for itself.

The light moved. Three inches across the stone. His right hand lay on the bench. The right hand still bore the mark of the wire, a thin crease on the palm where the barb had caught. She did not look at the hand. She looked at the water.

"It's cold now," she said. "By October it stops being a lake and becomes a fact."

His fingers were cold. The autumn at altitude, the drop in temperature between afternoon and four o'clock. Her hands on the book showed no vasoconstriction, the fingertips pink, the circulation of someone who had dressed for the cold she expected.

"Have you been here a long time?" "Always," she said. "Basel is an hour. This is here. I come here when the lake is becoming a fact."

"When it's cold." "When it stops accepting the boats." It was the right answer. Not the answer he had expected. "Why do you keep coming back?" "Because it doesn't ask me anything," she said.

A restaurant in Montreux, a Tuesday. She ordered for both of them because his French was medical French, anatomy and pathology, not the French of menus. She chose without consulting the card, her hand waving the waiter away with the ease of a woman who had eaten here before and would eat here again. The bread arrived in a basket. She tore it rather than cutting it, the French way, casual, one-handed, the thenar eminence doing the work, the crust fracturing cleanly along its weakest grain. He watched her hands tear the bread.

She talked about Basel. Her work, something in administration, he did not retain the details because the details were not the point. The point was her saying ordinary things in a tone that expected nothing from him except that he sit across a table and eat bread and be present. She did not ask about the war. She did not ask about India. She asked him to pass the salt.

He passed the salt. The affair was conducted in the Swiss manner, discreetly, in restaurants and on walks along the lake and in the particular privacy that neutral countries afford. Her parents in Basel received the information of his existence with the measured tolerance of people whose tolerance had never been tested by a brown man at their daughter's table. He visited them once. The visit was polite. The politeness was a wall with flowers on it. Her mother's hands shook when she poured the coffee. The shaking was not age. The father's posture in the doorway, the shoulders braced against the frame, was the posture of a man holding open a door he wanted to close.

He was, for the first time since the recruiting office in London, something like happy.

THE FILE

Chapter 24

I

Order was Swiss. The British did not share it.

Lieutenant Colonel Henry Forbes VC arrived to interview him. Forbes was a tank commander who had won the Victoria Cross in North Africa, a genuine hero, a man whose courage was documented and decorated, and who had escaped to Switzerland by his own considerable efforts.

An office in Montreux. Forbes's office. The desk was wooden, the grain visible beneath the varnish. Two chairs. The sun through the window was afternoon sun, the sun that came from the far side of the lake and made the office difficult to see clearly into and out of. Glare. Mazumdar's eyes squinted. Forbes's did not.

"Tell me about Berlin." "I was taken to Berlin in June 1942. I was questioned. I refused all collaboration. I was returned to Colditz."

"What did they offer?" "Leadership of the Indian Legion. Money. Rank."

"And you refused." "Yes." Forbes leaned back. His chair creaked. A small sound, the sound of weight being redistributed. His uniform was pressed. The creases were sharp enough to draw blood. His face was the colour of a man who has spent his adult life directing machines toward other men and who has not questioned whether the directing was correct.

"Why?" Mazumdar did not answer immediately. The office was cool. The afternoon light had turned everything the colour of ash. Forbes's face was ash-coloured. The desk was ash-coloured. The papers on the desk were ash-coloured.

"Because I took an oath." "To whom? Certainly not to Bose." "To myself. To do no harm to men who had helped me. To not betray the army I served."

Forbes was silent. His fingers were drumming on the desk. One finger at a time. Thumb. Index. Middle. Ring. The rhythm was impatience expressed as percussion. The desk absorbed it. The desk spoke the language of impatience back to him.

"You understand we need to verify this." "Verify what?" "Your account. The facts." "The facts are what I've told you." "Mazumdar." Forbes's voice had changed. Not angry. Disappointed. The tone of refused kindness. "You're making this difficult."

"I'm not making this anything. I answered your questions."

Forbes stood. He walked to the window. The window was large. Beyond it, the lake was visible, the lake in its afternoon aspect, no longer the pale mirror of morning but a thing darker, a thing that had absorbed the light and was releasing it upward into the sky. The light was leaving the lake. It was becoming the fact Elianne had described — ceasing to be a vehicle, becoming simply the presence of water at altitude.

"The file will reflect," Forbes said, "that you were unhelpful."

He did not turn around. He spoke to the window. The window was the direction his voice took.

Mazumdar stood. The chair scraped. "I've answered every question you asked me," he said. Forbes did not turn. He remained at the window, a silhouette against the ash-coloured light, a shape that had weight but no features.

II

The letter went to London. It was filed in a document marked Z/240. The document was marked, Indian Subversion. The document contained a single line of assessment, *I cannot say that I took a liking to Mazumdar. Needlessly verbose and somewhat cantankerous.*

Keenness. The second officer used the word in a room with green walls. A room specifically designed to have no connection to the exterior world. No windows. Green walls. A desk. Two chairs facing the desk. Mazumdar in one chair. The officer in the other.

"You displayed no keenness," the officer said, "to discuss your meeting with Bose."

"I have discussed it."

"Not with enthusiasm. The Berlin visit was significant. The Germans don't arrange personal transport for men they intend merely to question."

The words were spoken slowly. As though Mazumdar was a child or was deaf or did not speak English. As though the words themselves, when extended, would become clear.

"I refused," Mazumdar said. "What did you refuse?" "Everything." "We find that hard to believe." "Believe what you like. The facts remain." The officer made a note. The note was brief. It was not attempting to capture the facts. It was capturing an impression: *this man is hiding what he has seen.*

Mazumdar knew the impression had been formed before he entered the room. The impression had been formed when the file was opened. The impression had been formed when the label *Indian Subversion* was applied to an officer who had starved himself sixteen days for the army the officers served, who had jumped from a moving train, who had been beaten by the Gestapo for refusing the collaboration these officers were now suggesting he had perhaps accepted.

"We need your cooperation," the officer said. "You have it." "We need you to acknowledge the significance of the visit."

"I acknowledge that it happened. I acknowledge that I refused."

The officer leaned back. His chair was the same chair Forbes's had been. Identical furniture, identical offices, identical men. The leaning back was the gesture of a third explanation being prepared, this time with reduced patience.

"Your service," the officer said, "depends on your cooperation."

Mazumdar did not respond. "Do you understand?" "I understand that you are suggesting my future depends on my agreeing with your conclusion about my past."

"Not agreeing. Being honest." "I have been honest." The officer made another note. Briefer than the first. The note was shorter because the assessment was hardening. The assessment was becoming, *this man is uncooperative.*

III

Lieutenant Colonel Sidney Lassiter of the 16th Punjab Regiment had been watching him for months.

The watching had the quality of observation, not investigation. Lassiter was hunting.

The ophthalmoscope arrived from Geneva on a Tuesday. It was carried in a leather case. The case was lined with velvet. The instrument itself was new, the lens clear, the light working when tested against the palm. Mazumdar signed for it. The receipt went into his pocket.

The summons came the next day. Lassiter's office was wooden. Not ash-coloured like Forbes's, the colour of wood that had been varnished repeatedly until the varnish had become the thing itself and had buried the original beneath it. The desk was large. It was positioned so that the light from the window behind it would render the face of the man sitting across from it in shadow. Lassiter was aware of this.

"You're a bloody liar, Mazumdar."

The words arrived without preamble. Without greeting. Without the interval that usually separates two men entering a room from the beginning of conversation. The words were the beginning of the conversation.

Mazumdar remained standing. "Colonel." "Sit." He sat. The chair was smaller than Lassiter's. The chair was angled so that Lassiter could look down at him.

"You didn't buy that instrument." "I did." "The money was stolen. The girl in Geneva, she has signed a statement. She never sold you anything."

Mazumdar reached into his pocket. The ophthalmoscope was in his jacket, in its case, not his pocket. The receipt was in his pocket. He removed it. The receipt was printed. It had a number on it. The number matched the serial number engraved on the ophthalmoscope. The matching was precise. The precision was the sort of precision that only facts could produce.

Lassiter did not look at the receipt. His eyes remained on Mazumdar's face.

"The girl was mistaken," Mazumdar said. "The girl was pressured. And you were the one who pressured her."

"I have never met the girl. I ordered the instrument by telephone. I retrieved it in person. I signed for it with a chit from the senior medical officer."

Lassiter stood. He walked around the desk. The walking was the preparation for violence, though the violence would not be physical. Lassiter had learned in India that violence could be administered without touching. The violence could be administered through words. Through documents. Through files.

"Do you know what happens to men who lie to the army?"

Mazumdar did not answer. "Men who betray their oath. Men who steal. Men who consort with the enemy and then come back and lie about it."

"I haven't done any of those things." "You have done all of them." Lassiter was pacing now. The pacing was part of the architecture. The pacing was the movement of a man constructing a case in his mind, invisible, that would be difficult to dismantle once it had been constructed.

"Four years in India," Lassiter said. "I know how you people think. I know what you're capable of. You arrive in Europe speaking your proper English, and then when you think no one is watching, you drop the mask and you show what you really are."

"What am I really, Colonel?" The masseter. The quarter-millimetre. The jaw performing the same contraction it had performed in the courtyard at Colditz, in the kitchen, in the corridor outside the washroom. The body's oldest answer to the body's oldest insult.

"A liar. A thief. A man who cannot be trusted." "Then why am I not in a cell?" The question hung in the room. The asking changed Lassiter's face. Anger gave way to calculation.

"You soon will be. I'm having you charged. Theft. Deception. Insubordination."

Both men were on their feet. Lassiter went from pink to purple, the progression visible in real time, the blood rising through the colonel's neck and into his face.

"The difference between you and me, Colonel, is this: You have lived in my country for twenty-five years and you can't speak one of its languages. I have lived in your country for fifteen and speak five languages, including yours."

The room was silent. Lassiter's face was purple. The purple was not anger now.

Mazumdar stood. The chair scraped. "I have the receipt, Colonel." He placed the receipt on the desk. The serial number faced upward. He walked to the door and opened it, walked through it and did not close it behind him.

Lassiter's face changed. The purple drained from it. The face became the colour of ash.

IV

They placed him under house arrest.

A hotel room in Locarno. The window opened. The lake was visible. The Swiss would not permit a cell — they permitted observation, restriction, surveillance, but not imprisonment. The distinction was important to the Swiss. The distinction meant they were different from the Germans. They were proving it by means of a room with a view.

Four months. The mattress was soft. His body could not recalibrate to softness. The body had been trained in resistance, in the hard surfaces of stone and wire. Softness was disorientation. He woke with his spine aching, the ache the ache of the body demanding resistance from the world around it, the resistance no longer being available.

Nobody. The sentence was his. Spoken later, to the tape recorder. *I had nobody to help me.* The people who might have helped, the officers at the club, the other escaped men, Hammond, were the same people who had engineered the help to fail. The system was the system that was prosecuting him. The oath was the oath he had sworn to that system. The system had the oath. The oath could not protect him from the system.

The receipt was in his pocket. The ophthalmoscope was in his room. The serial numbers matched. The facts remained facts.

Then a Swiss colonel came to see him. The colonel was the senior Swiss officer overseeing British servicemen in the region. His uniform was pressed but not sharp. The pressing was functional. The uniform was a fact of his employment, not an assertion. He sat in the chair beside the window. His spine was straight but not rigid. He did not lean backward. He sat as though sitting were a neutral act, neither domination nor submission.

"Tell me," the Swiss colonel said. Mazumdar told him. The ophthalmoscope. The chit. The receipt. The false statement. The girl who had been pressured. The four months.

“They want me struck from the medical register,” Mazumdar said. “They want to ruin me.”

The Swiss colonel listened. His face did not change. The absence of judgment. The absence of the question that was waiting beneath every conversation: *But why are you here?*

“I can arrange a transfer,” the Swiss colonel said. “A nursing home. Outside his jurisdiction.”

“He has the rank to follow.” “He does. I have the authority to stop it.” He arranged the transfer. The transfer came through. A nursing home in the mountains, higher than Montreux, higher than Locarno, high enough that the air changed and the temperature dropped and the light became clearer. He was removed. The file remained. The file was noted, *Case transferred to Swiss civilian authority. Prosecution suspended pending review.*

The review would never conclude. The review would be suspended, the suspension would become permanent. The file would remain marked Indian Subversion for as long as files were kept, and then it would be classified and the classified would become declassified and the declassified would become historical. The ophthalmoscope would remain in his room. The receipt would remain in his pocket. The serial numbers would never be questioned again because the question had been asked and had been answered and the answer had been: *not this man, not this moment, not this war.*

V

In November 1944 they transferred him to Marseille and put him on a troop ship bound for England. The crossing was slow and the sea was grey and the ship was full of men going home from the war and the going-home had a quality he shared and did not share, shared because England was where he was going, did not share because England was not home, had never been home, was the country whose oath he had kept and whose officers had tried to court-martial him for keeping it.

Woolwich barracks. Two weeks. Then a summons to the War Office.

The debriefing was in a room with green walls, a desk, two officers with files. They asked questions and he answered them. Colditz, the layout, the guard rotations, the escape routes he had observed. He told them about the Indian camp. He told them about the wire.

One of the officers turned a page. "You were taken to Berlin in June 1942. Can you tell us about that visit?"

He opened his mouth. The room was warm and the officers were patient, the file was open and the space for the answer was there, on the page, waiting. He could have said the name. Bose. He could have described the dinner, the fish, the Bengali, the handshake, the refusal. The words were available.

"I was questioned and returned to Colditz." The answer came simply.

The officer made a note. The note was brief. The file on the desk was labelled with a designation he would later learn was Z/240. Indian Subversion. The file contained Forbes's letter (*the behaviour of Captain Mazumdar gave rise to suspicion*) and the MI5 officer's own assessment, which would be declassified decades later, *Z/240 was very hard to deal with. He disliked being interviewed and expressed the opinion that he was being subjected to treatment that no British POW had to put up with.*

The other officer spoke. "Your file has been flagged, Dr Mazumdar. Berlin arranged personal transport for you. The Germans don't arrange personal transport for men they intend to merely question."

The sentence hung in the room the way diagnoses hang in consulting rooms, conclusions reached before the patient was asked to sit down.

"I refused," he said. Later, the MI5 file would note, *It seems impossible that Z/240 has forgotten as much as he pretends.*

The officer who had spoken leaned forward. "You understand, Dr Mazumdar, that your cooperation in this matter affects how your service is recognised. You are ruining your chances of getting a medal."

"Do you think I escaped and went through all these things just to get a bloody medal?"

He shouted it. The shouting surprised him, the volume arriving from a place the clinical voice did not control. The officers' faces changed. He stood. He walked out.

They assigned him quarters. They gave him back pay for three years of captivity.

He was free. The freedom was large and empty. He booked passage to India.

SHABASH

Chapter 25

I

1946. The house was smaller than he remembered.

This was the thought that arrived first, the house was smaller, the walls lower, the courtyard narrower, the mango tree reduced from the immensity of childhood to a tree that was simply a tree. He stood in the entrance. He had last walked through it at seventeen, going the other way, going out, going to London. The same doorway. The man who stood in it was not.

In the house, Bhola's wife and children in the rooms that had been their father's rooms, in the kitchen that had been their mother's kitchen. A child's toy, a wooden horse, small, painted blue, sat on the step where his father's sandals used to sit.

Bhola came to the doorway. His brother's face. He knew from the face. The particular arrangement of features was not surprise, not grief, not welcome. It was something else, the look a face gets when it must tell a thing that has been true for years and has not yet been said. Bhola's eyes moved from his face to his uniform and back to his face.

"Baba is gone." Gone. Not dead, gone. *Chole gechen.* The Bengali word carried the euphemism of a language that treats death as departure, as though the dead have simply left for a journey.

In the doorway. The wooden horse on the step. The mango tree. The courtyard where the light fell.

His hands were steady. He noted this the way he noted everything — from outside, from the place where observation lived.

"When?" Bhola told him. During the war. He did not hear the specific year or the specific month because what was relevant was that the death had occurred while he was somewhere else, in a castle or a train or a room in Berlin or a barn in France, and during every one of those places his father had been dead and he had not known.

You only shave your head when your father or mother dies.

The words arrived from Kassel. From the morning when they had tried to shave his head and he had refused because his father was alive. His father had been dead. The ritual he had defended was already owed.

Inside. He sat in a chair that was not his father's chair. The room smelled of someone else's cooking and someone else's soap and children.

Tea, from his mother. She was alive. She was smaller than he remembered, a woman who had been formidable now moved slowly, her hands shaking slightly as she held the cup. Her eyes, when they found his face, contained a recognition not of the man he was but of the boy he had been.

Tea in his hands. He drank it. He did not speak about his father.

He stood. The house had a pulse, children's voices in the back room, the scrape of a pot on the stove, Bhola's voice, low and steady, speaking to his wife. Mazumdar moved through the rooms he had been born in. The parlour first, the furniture different, arranged for a family of five instead of four. The books his father had kept on the east wall were gone. Their dust pattern remained on the shelf, a precise shadow of his father's reading.

To the surgery. The room had not changed in structure. The window still faced the street. The shelves still climbed the north wall. But the surgical instruments, the scalpels, the forceps, the dissecting needles in their leather roll, his father's instruments, the ones that had opened two thousand bodies in this room, tools that were his father's hands extended, they were gone. In their place, Bhola's medical texts. A stethoscope coiled on the desk like a snake, recognising itself. The leather chair where his father had sat taking histories was now a wooden chair with a rush seat, the kind a village doctor might use.

One object remained. On the lowest shelf, pushed toward the back where the light did not reach, a wooden chest, not large, with brass corners corroded to a pale green. His father's instrument chest from medical school, Edinburgh, 1902. The initials carved into the lid had been deepened over the years to prevent their erasure.

He did not touch it. He stood in the surgery, the room that had been the house's essential organ, and understood that a man can remain alive in memory while every evidence of his hands is being replaced. The Upanayana thread the Brahmin had placed on his shoulder at age eleven had been torn from him during the delousing at Kassel. His father's instruments had migrated from this room. Both were gone. Both were in a place where no one could follow.

The children's voices moved through the house. A child, he did not know which child, was laughing.

Chair. Tea. Outside, the mango tree was simply a tree and somewhere beyond the walls the Phalgu ran underground, the surface dry and quiet and giving no sign.

II

The morning of departure was hot as Bihar mornings in early summer are hot, with the humid weight of a season that has not yet committed to monsoon, pressing against the skin and the lungs and the cotton of a British uniform designed for a different climate.

He bought first-class tickets for the Calcutta train. Two for his brother's family and one for himself.

Gaya Junction. He knew this station from inside, from the body's memory, the quality of light on the platform and the smell of coal smoke, frying oil and the sound of chai-wallahs calling in voices that had not changed since his childhood. Samosas in oil. Pakoras on newspaper. The sweet heaviness of jalebi cooling on a metal tray. Hindi and Magahi and the occasional sharp Bengali of a traveller from Calcutta. Porters in red turbans. A dog sleeping on the platform.

He installed his brother's family in their first-class compartment. He arranged the bags. He told them he would return with food. He walked the platform toward the vendors.

Samosas. The oil stained through the newspaper wrapping, warm against his fingers, the pastry crisp and ridged where the edges had been crimped by the vendor's thumb. He bit into one as he walked, the shell shattering, the filling hot and dense with potato and cumin and green chilli, the chilli hitting the back of his throat with a sharpness that made his eyes water, and the watering was recognition. This taste. This heat. He bought chai in small clay cups, rough and cool in his palm. The chai sweet, milky, thick with cardamom. He bought bananas for the children. He carried the food back along the platform.

III

The compartment was not empty.

Thirty yards away, the open door, a shape in the corridor, the angle of a man's body blocking the entrance. Then his sister-in-law's voice, the children's, and a voice he did not recognise, English, male.

Bhola met him on the platform. His brother's face, the face of humiliation.

"What happened?" "They told me to get out." A British sergeant major. Making way for an Englishman and his mistress who required the first-class compartment more than the Indian family holding first-class tickets.

Something opened. To the compartment. The sergeant major was standing in the corridor, thick-necked, red-faced, sweating in the heat.

"Stand to attention." The voice that came from Mazumdar was not the voice of the room in Berlin. It was the voice of a man who had carried the oath for seven years and who was now, on a platform in Gaya, using it.

"Stand to attention! Salute a senior officer!" The sergeant major's face changed. The change moved through surprise and confusion and arrived at fear. The sergeant was looking at the pips. At the King's Commission on the shoulder of the brown-skinned man who outranked him.

The sergeant stood to attention. His heels came together. His hands went to his sides. His chin rose.

Mazumdar spoke. He spoke for several minutes. He did not remember, later, the specific words, the words were the vehicle for the thing that was being released, and the thing was seven years.

"You are dismissed." The sergeant went. The Englishman and his mistress went. The first-class seats were available again.

Turned. The platform was silent. The porters had dropped their bundles. The chai-wallahs had stopped calling. The vendors had lowered their trays. A thousand people were staring at the Indian officer in the British uniform who had just made a British sergeant stand to attention and salute and leave.

Then the sound. It did not begin everywhere at once. It began, he would remember this, would carry this specific detail through fifty years and into a recording in a room in Devon, it began with applause. A single pair of hands. Then another. Then the stamping of feet, bare feet and sandalled feet and the heavy boots of porters and the quick hard slap of children's feet on the platform, and the stamping built and the applause built and the two sounds merged into a roar that came from the crowd and hit him in the chest the way the heat from the burning ambulance had hit him in France, as a physical surface, and on the other side of the surface was a voice. A child's voice. A boy near the chai-wallah's cart, barefoot on the platform, eight or ten, who said the word before the adults did.

"Shabash!" The word erupted from the crowd: plural, anonymous, a wave. *Shabash. Shabash. Shabash.* Bravo. Well done. The Hindi that every person on that platform shared with every other person and that he shared with them and that was not the language of the oath and not the language of the institution and not the language that the Royal College had taught him or the King's Commission had given him but the language of the place where he was born, the language of the platform, the language that rose from the crowd and wrapped around him and was, for the duration of the sound, the only language in the world.

On the platform. The crowd roared. The samosas were still in his hand, the paper wrapping darkened with oil, warm against his palm. The word was in the air and the word was *Shabash* and it meant *bravo* and it meant *we saw you* and none of them knew what he had done, not the tanks, not the handkerchief, not the castle, not Bose's coffee, not the sixteen days, not the wire, not the 900 kilometres, they knew only what they had seen, an Indian officer who had made a British sergeant stand to attention. And that was enough.

IV

Back into the compartment, his brother's family reinstalled. He gave them the samosas and the chai.

The train left. He watched it go. On the platform he remained until it emptied. The porters returned to their bundles. The vendors resumed their calls. The dog put its head back down.

He left the station. He walked through Gaya. Somewhere to the east the Phalgu ran underground. He did not go to the river. He did not go to the Vishnupad Temple. The time for the rituals had passed.

He returned to England. The ship crossed water for fourteen days. At night the phosphorescence broke along the bow, the deck tilted beneath him, the distance between the ocean liner and the platform at Gaya Junction became measurable, then immeasurable. The word *Shabash* sank slowly, the sound growing fainter the way sounds grow faint underwater, until even the memory of it became a motion, not a voice, but the wake of a voice already gone.

SECTION II

THE SILENCE

THE RADIO

Chapter 26

I

He had been in Cardiff for two years when the radio changed.

August the fifteenth, 1947. He was making tea. On the gas ring, the kettle. In the kitchen of the house in Cardiff where he rented two rooms, a bedroom and a sitting room. There was a gas ring and a sink and a window. Through the window, a yard. In the yard, a neighbour's sheets hung in perpetual laundry. The sheets were white. They moved in the wind, the only life visible from the window. The kettle was metal, heavy, the weight familiar in his hand. The gas ring was blue when it ignited, the flame responding immediately to the turn of the knob. These were small facts, small technologies, but they were present in his hand every morning and the presence mattered.

On, always on, the radio. He kept it on, because the sound filled the room. The radio spoke in BBC English and the BBC English had a quality he depended upon, measured, impersonal.

He was pouring water into the pot when the voice changed.

Not the words, the voice changed first. A formality entered the broadcast that was different from the usual formality, the way a doctor's voice changes when the diagnosis is no longer routine, and his hand stopped moving, the kettle suspended above the pot, the steam rising into his face with a heat that was, for a half-second, his mother's kitchen in Gaya. Then Cardiff again.

India was free. The words arrived in the room carrying information that had already happened elsewhere. The ceremonies in Delhi, the midnight session, the speeches, the flag, had happened while he slept in Cardiff in a rented room above a yard. The freedom had been declared in Hindi and in English and he had not been among the millions who heard it because he was here, in Wales, making tea.

Down went the kettle, still warm. He turned off the radio. He turned it back on. The radio continued its speech but the words were behind him now, trailing. He filled the sink. He washed the teacup. He placed it on the shelf, the cup aligned with the other cups, the shelf organised, the small geometry of domestic objects maintained. The washing required his hands. The hands continued with their work. The kitchen continued with its morning.

He stood at the window. He drank the tea, watching the sheets. English tea: no cardamom, no ginger, no elaichi crushed between the teeth. The cardamom had run out and not been replaced. The jaggery substituted for sugar. The steel tumbler for a china cup. The radio said India and the word was a tightening across his chest where the sacred thread had once rested. His fingers ached around the cup, the left hand, the metacarpal that had broken on the rail tie near Angoulême, the joint stiff in the mornings now, the body carrying the escape in its bones.

II

What he had not known, what everyone had known and no one had said clearly enough, was that the freedom would arrive with a knife. Partition. The word meant what it said, a cutting, a division. Punjab divided. Bengal divided. Twelve million people moving in columns, not unlike the column he had walked in seven years earlier, from Étaples to Kassel, except that this column moved in two directions and the people in it were citizens of countries that had not existed the day before.

He read the newspapers with the attention of a doctor reading case notes. The photographs. The columns of refugees. The bodies in the roads. Punjab, the word hit him each time because Punjab was not abstract. Punjab was Singh.

Dariao Singh. Hands the size of soup plates. The man who had pulled Mazumdar up an eighteen-foot gate as though lifting a child. The man who had walked nine hundred kilometres without complaint.

Singh was from Punjab. Punjab was burning. He did not know if Singh was alive. He had not known since Switzerland, since the separation. He had not tried to find him. The not-trying was a knowledge that the finding would produce one of two results, both unbearable.

He set the newspaper down. He washed the teacup. He dried it and placed it on the shelf, the cup aligned with the other cups, the order maintained.

III

Already happened, the INA Trials.

The Red Fort trials, Delhi, November 1945: three officers in the dock, a Hindu, a Muslim, a Sikh. The charges, waging war against the

King-Emperor. The same King-Emperor to whom Mazumdar had sworn his oath.

He read the proceedings in the *Times*. He read them standing at the counter of a newsagent in Cardiff, his coat damp from the walk, his fingers leaving prints on the page. Colonel Prem Kumar Sahgal, Major General Shah Nawaz Khan, Colonel Gurbaksh Singh Dhillon. Three men who had worn the same uniform, eaten the same rations, recited the same oath, and then had walked into Bose's army and fought against the men they had trained with. The photographs showed them in the dock: composed, thin, not yet aware that the trial would make them.

Nehru himself stood as defence counsel. Nehru, whom Mazumdar had seen once, at a distance, in Calcutta in 1937, a slim figure in white speaking from a platform. Now Nehru was in court arguing that the three officers had followed their conscience, that the oath to the King-Emperor was an oath extracted under colonial coercion, that the real treason was the Empire's treatment of its Indian subjects.

Mazumdar set the newspaper down. He picked it up again.

The prosecution's argument was precise, clinical, an argument he understood in his bones because the same precision governed his own life. An oath was an oath. The oath did not ask whether the swearer agreed with the cause. The oath asked only that the swearer hold. Sahgal had not held. Khan had not held. Dhillon had not held. They had broken, and the breaking, regardless of its moral content, was a breaking.

Acquittals. The officers were released. The *Times* carried photographs the next day. Shah Nawaz carried shoulder-high through the Red Fort gates, the crowd surging around him, garlands piling at his neck until the garlands obscured his chest. Dhillon weeping. Sahgal's wife pushing through the crowd to reach him, her sari pulled across her face against the dust, and the reaching, a woman's arm through a crowd of ten thousand, producing in Mazumdar's chest a contraction that he diagnosed as intercostal muscle spasm and that was not intercostal muscle spasm.

The Congress adopted them. Their faces were in every newspaper. The faces were the faces of men who looked like him, Indian officers, King's commissioned, same training, same war, except that these men had made the opposite choice and the opposite choice had made them national heroes and his choice had made him a man standing in a newsagent in Cardiff reading about heroes he was not.

The mutinies followed. The Royal Indian Navy. Bombay, February 1946. Ratings on twenty ships striking, the Congress flag raised on the masts. The connection between the Red Fort verdicts and the ratings' courage was a line drawn in public, the INA officers had proved that the oath could be broken and the breaking honoured. The British saw it. The transfer of power accelerated. The men who had joined Bose, the men Mazumdar had refused to join, had helped to end the Empire.

No arithmetic. He did not calculate what his own refusal had or had not accomplished. The refusal was a fact, he had said no and the no was as final as a surgical incision, it could not be undone, the tissue could not be reattached. But the fact existed now inside a context that had not existed in the room in Berlin, and the context changed the fact's weight without changing the fact itself.

He folded the newspaper. He placed it on the counter. He walked to the hospital.

In the corridor a colleague, an English surgeon, the man cheerful, competent, incurious, asked Mazumdar if he had followed the news from India. Mazumdar said he had. The colleague said it was a shame about the Empire but probably inevitable. The colleague said this while scrubbing his hands at the basin, the soap lathering, the water running. Mazumdar watched the man's hands under the water. Clean, pink, confident hands that had never held a baton before a line of tanks.

"Probably," Mazumdar said. He walked to the ward. A patient, a miner with pneumoconiosis, the lungs silted with decades of coal dust, was waiting for his rounds. The miner's chest X-ray was on the lightbox. Mazumdar studied it, the opacities, the fibrosis, thirty years of coal dust in the lungs. He held the X-ray to the light and the light passed through the healthy tissue and stopped at the scarred tissue and the distinction between what the light passed through and what it did not was the distinction between the life the man had lived and the life the man would live, and the reading of this distinction was Mazumdar's work, and the work held.

IV

Bose was dead.

He had learned this two years earlier, from a newspaper at a bus stop in London. The headline contained Bose's name and the word *dead*. The reading of it produced a response he had not anticipated, a stillness, a held breath, and then a release, of a tension held since the room in Berlin, since the handshake, since the corridor he had chosen not to walk down.

Subhas Chandra Bose had died, or had reportedly died, the reports already contradicting each other, in a plane crash in Taiwan on August the eighteenth. The man who had sat across from him and said *When you change your mind, we will be here* had not lived to see the India he had tried to create.

The bus came. He got on. He rode it to his quarters.

V

Not on August the fifteenth. The silence had begun earlier.

It had begun at the War Office, when the officer behind the desk had looked at his file and looked at him. The officer had been polite. *Credit for remaining loyal.* The words had landed with the weight of an insult wrapped in a compliment, because *credit* was the language of accounting, not of sacrifice, and *remaining loyal* implied that disloyalty had been the expected outcome.

The door had closed behind him. The corridor was long. His footsteps made no sound on it.

By August 1947, the silence was two years old. It had formed around the war the way calcium forms around a foreign body, slowly, the encasement becoming harder each month until the thing inside was no longer a wound but a structure.

And now Partition had completed the architecture. The oath attached him to a country that had just divided his country with a line drawn by a man who had never been to India, a boundary sketched in six weeks by Cyril Radcliffe in a bungalow in Delhi.

He stood at the window in Cardiff. The sheets on the line had dried. The radio had moved on. The tea was cold in his hand.

Down the sink went the tea. He rinsed the cup. He placed it on the shelf. He went to the hospital.

The silence held.

THE COUNTER

Chapter 27

I

He met Ruth in a bank.

He was at the counter. The war had been over three years. The return to medicine was the return to the self that existed before convoy, tanks, and castle. He was completing his surgical qualifications, the captivity had interrupted, the debriefing had extended the interruption, and the body had recovered. But the architecture behind the body had been rearranged.

He dressed as if dressing were a discipline. Waistcoat buttoned, jacket pressed, shoes polished to the standard of someone who had once had nothing, not even shoes. The gloves were leather, dark, worn indoors and out, and he would not smoke without them.

Ruth was the cashier. She would remember the gloves first. Then the posture, a man standing at a bank counter as if the standing were a form of attention, the weight evenly distributed, the patience held, active. What she saw was the stillness. As though every part of him had been considered and arranged.

She noticed him. He noticed that she noticed. A second look. Then a third. Then a conversation outside the bank about nothing that mattered, the weather, the town, the tedium of Wednesday afternoons.

II

The courtship was walks. England in 1948, the country tired, the buildings still scarred, the rationing still in force, and walking cost nothing. They walked along the Taff in the evenings after her shift at the bank and his shift at the hospital.

The stares came. He was practised at the stares. Seven years of being stared at had made him expert in the art of moving through attention without acknowledging it. Ruth was not practised. She was defiant — with the quiet stubbornness of a woman who had decided what she wanted and would not undecide it because strangers disapproved. She walked beside him.

"You don't talk about the war," she said. This was their fourth meeting. They were drinking tea in a café near the bank.

"No." "That's all right." "Is it?" "My brother doesn't talk about it either. He was at Arnhem."

She said this without expectation, a declaration of understanding. She had lived beside silence before. She knew its dimensions. Her brother had come home from Arnhem, had not spoken about Arnhem. The not-speaking had become part of the house, and the family had accommodated it the way a house accommodates a room that is kept locked, by walking past the door, by learning not to try the handle.

They married in 1950. Registry office. Small. His father was dead. Mazumdar did not say this and Ruth did not know it. Ruth's parents came. Her father shook Mazumdar's hand with the grip of someone with opinions about the marriage who had chosen not to voice them. Her mother wore a hat and smiled; the hat was new, the smile not quite.

The door to the registry office opened. They stepped into the street. It rained.

II-A

A walk. The Taff in November. The light failing early, four o'clock and the sky already a sheet of grey above the river, the water dark, the trees bare. Ruth wore a coat that was too thin for the wind. She did not mention the cold. He noticed it, her shoulders drawing inward, the slight contraction of her frame, and he removed his jacket and placed it across her shoulders without speaking.

She looked at him. The jacket was warm from his body. "You'll freeze." "I have a waistcoat." "A waistcoat isn't a coat." "A waistcoat is adequate." She laughed. The laughter was sudden, unplanned, and it carried across the river in the still air. A man walking his dog on the far bank looked up. The man looked at them, a brown man in a waistcoat, a fair-haired woman in a man's jacket, and the looking lasted three seconds and Ruth, who had noticed the looking, did not alter her stride.

They walked. The path along the Taff was mud in places. The mud had a smell he had not encountered since France — cold iron, wet leaves, the particular sweetness of a river in autumn. He offered his arm; she took it — practical, functional, a woman accepting assistance on uneven ground. But the arm remained after the ground levelled. She did not release it. He did not withdraw it.

"My mother wants to know what you do." "I'm a surgeon." "She wants to know what kind." "General. I'm completing the fellowship." "She wants to know where you trained." "Edinburgh." "She wants to know where you're from." The pause. Not a refusal, a gathering. He looked at the river. The water moved slowly, the colour of tea, carrying leaves and small branches from the upstream woods.

"Bihar. A city called Gaya. It is in the east of India, near the Ganges plain."

"Is it beautiful?" He considered this. The question required an answer that was not a medical answer, not a factual answer. It required an answer from a part of him that the war had cauterised and the cauterisation had been so thorough that the question, *is it beautiful,* arrived at a surface that could not receive it.

"There is a river," he said. "The Phalgu. It runs through the city but for most of the year the riverbed is dry. The water runs underground. You can see the sand and the stones, the people walking across the bed, and beneath them the river is flowing, and you cannot see it."

Ruth looked at him. She did not ask what this had to do with beauty. She had a quality he would spend forty-six years in its company recognising.

"Like the Taff in summer," she said.

"Not like the Taff." "No. Not like the Taff." They walked on. The dog walker had gone. The path narrowed between the river and a wall of blackthorn, and they walked single file for twenty yards and then the path widened again and she found his arm again and the finding was a continuation, the arm there, the hand there, the warmth of a man's body conducted through wool into her fingers.

At the bridge she stopped. She took his jacket from her shoulders and held it out to him. He took it. Their hands touched during the exchange, his fingers against hers, the contact brief, the temperature of her skin registering against his with the precision of a clinical thermometer.

"Thursday?" she said. "Thursday." She crossed the bridge. He watched her walk, the stride even, the coat too thin, the fair hair catching the last of the light. She did not look back. This was a quality he recognised from the army, the discipline of the forward gaze, the refusal to check whether you were being watched.

He put on his jacket. It smelled faintly of her: soap, wool, a warmth that was not his warmth.

He walked to his lodgings. He made tea. He stood at the window and drank it. The tea was hot, the room cold, the river out there in the dark, running.

III

They moved to Wales. The practice was in a town near the coast, a surgery on the ground floor of a building that smelled of disinfectant and carbolic soap. The smell was familiar. Edinburgh had smelled this way, the anatomy hall, the teaching hospital. The smell was associated in his body with precision, with learning, with the work of healing. He hung his diplomas. FRCS, Royal College of Surgeons of Edinburgh, Diploma in Tropical Medicine. The frames were new. The man behind them had been stripped naked at Kassel.

The patients came. Some put it down. He saw it, the pause at the door, the recalibration when the face behind the desk was not the face they expected. A woman asked the receptionist whether there was *another* doctor. A man directed his complaints to the wall behind Mazumdar's head. A farmer brought his son and held the boy's arm while Mazumdar examined it, the holding protective in a way that exceeded the medical context.

Most came back. He was thorough. He listened, with the same sustained observation that had been his only private act in five years of captivity. He made house calls in the rain, carried his bag to farmhouses on hills where the wind came from the sea and the stairs were narrow, the patient was old and the only treatment was presence, to sit beside the bed, hold the wrist, count the pulse.

Secrets, their secrets. A man who could not speak about his own history spent forty years listening to others speak about theirs. The woman who wept about her marriage. The farmer who drank, it was in his liver. The teenager who had done something and the something was in the blood test, the file was in the drawer and the drawer was locked. His medical bag sat in the corner of the consulting room: leather, worn, lighter now than it had been in France because it contained fewer instruments, but still substantial, still requiring his hand to grip it, still present in his arms when he made a house call, the familiar weight a grounding against the unreality of conversation.

Ruth ran the practice, the appointments, the accounts, the correspondence. She had a voice for the telephone that was brisk and warm at once, and patients sometimes asked for her by name when they rang, not him. She managed him too, his handwriting was dreadful, and she transcribed his notes into the ledger each evening at the kitchen table, her hands moving across the page with the precise neatness of a woman trained in the discipline of a bank counter, the writing aligned, the ledger balanced. Occasionally she queried a dosage. She was usually right. He would look at her over his glasses and say nothing, and she would pencil in the correction without comment, her hand reaching for the pencil with the same certainty she reached for everything, the teacup, the door latch, his arm in the dark.

She learned when to speak and when not to. She learned that the nights were difficult. Her hand found his forearm in the dark, not pressing, not asking, just the palm resting against his skin. The gesture would last forty-six years.

IV

The sons arrived.

Ashok first. Born in 1952. The boy was small and dark-haired and his face was both of them, Ruth's jaw, Mazumdar's brow.

Mazumdar held him. The hands that had held a baton before twenty German tanks, that had gripped the wire until it cut through the gloves, that had carried their own starving body through sixteen days, the hands held a child who weighed seven pounds.

He chose the name. Ashok, *without sorrow* in Sanskrit. Ruth said the name, *Ashok*. Her English mouth shaped the syllables with the careful approximation of a woman learning a word in a language she would never speak, and the approximation was close enough.

Kamal came two years later. Darker than Ashok, quieter, with eyes that followed his father around the room with an attention that Mazumdar recognised, his own. Kamal, *lotus*.

Bengali names in a Welsh town. The names in the other children's mouths: mispronounced, shortened, adapted, the Sanskrit rhythms flattened by English tongues until the names that had meant *without sorrow* and *lotus* meant nothing at all, a river going underground, and when you look down the water is gone.

He did not teach them Bengali. The language lived in Gaya, and Gaya was the place where his father was dead and the platform was where he had last heard the word *Shabash* from strangers who did not know what he had done. The boys spoke English. They grew up in a house where the kitchen smelled of Ruth's cooking, shepherd's pie, Sunday roasts. Mazumdar ate everything. He cleaned the plate. He used bread to wipe the last trace from the china. Ruth found this endearing. She did not know it was a hunger strike thing.

He cooked sometimes. Sundays, when Ruth rested. He made dal, the spices arriving from a shop in Cardiff, the cumin and turmeric and coriander measured into his palm with the precision of a man weighing anaesthetic, the quantities exact, his mother's quantities, scripture. The dal simmered. The house filled with a smell that was Gaya, the past.

Ruth tasted the dal. She ate it carefully. She said it was good. It was good.

The boys ate it too. They ate it with bread, not rice.

IV-A

Sunday morning. Ashok was at the kitchen table, six years old, dark hair falling across his forehead, drawing something with a pencil, careful lines, deliberate, the tip of his tongue pressed against his upper lip where concentration went.

Mazumdar was at the stove. A cast-iron pot, heavy, its surface burnished by decades, his mother's pot, shipped with other surviving things. Water beginning its climb. He would wait for the boil. He waited with the patience that Ruth observed in him and called grace but that was only the discipline of five years learning that hurrying changed nothing, that time unrushed carried the same weight as time panicked, and that standing with weight distributed equally between both feet was a form of prayer.

The cumin seeds arrived first. They crackled, a sound like small bones. Ashok looked up.

"What are you making?" "Dal. Lentils. Your mother's mother's mother made this in Gaya."

The boy did not know Gaya. Gaya was a sound, a syllable with no country attached. He returned to his drawing.

Mazumdar measured the turmeric. His palm open, the powder orange-red, the specific shade of *alta* dye, the colour that had not changed in his memory. One quarter teaspoon. The measurement was his mother's measurement. The powder descended into heat. The smell rose, not sweet, not sharp, but the precision of loss, the way a kitchen remembers the hands that once commanded it. Not grief. The chemistry of a spice dissolving into oil.

"Can I stir?"

Ashok had slipped down from his chair and was standing now, not quite to the height of the stove, his small face tilted upward, the attention in his eyes the same attention Mazumdar had trained upon the world for seven years, the cataloguing gaze, the refusal to miss what was happening.

Mazumdar reached for him. He lifted, that specific weight, that particular density of a six-year-old body that he would hold in his hands for exactly one decade before the boy's own skeleton would lengthen and harden and the child-weight would vanish forever. The boy's feet cleared the floor. He was held level to the stove.

Ashok's hands — the fingers small, the fingernails pale crescents, the palm still smooth, still unmarked by the year-by-year abrasion of living, reached for the wooden spoon. His wrist was thin as a bird's. Mazumdar's own hand did not release the boy's arm; he held it steady while the child stirred, the movements tentative, the lentils beginning their dark congregation.

The boy breathed. Shallow, rapid, concentration's breathing, of a small effort performed in the presence of a taller person. Mazumdar noted this with the part of his mind that catalogued the physiological: tachycardia of focus, not fear. Healthy. Normal. The body learning its own capacities.

"Good," Mazumdar said. The boy stirred. The dal darkened. "My mother made this," Mazumdar said. "In Gaya. Every Sunday."

The boy did not ask what Gaya was. He had learned, early, that his father spoke sometimes in the pluperfect tense, in had-beens and no-longers, and that the words that followed carried a weight that required no answer. He stirred. The spoon moved through the thickening golden-orange, and the smell rose between them, warm, absolute, indifferent to all history.

Mazumdar held his son level to the stove for as long as the stirring took. His arms did not tire. He did not set the boy down. He held him, this boy who would grow to be a man in a country that would never be his country, who would carry his father's name past the syllables into the flattened English pronunciation, held him in the steam, in the spice-smell, in the moment before language would arrive to explain it away.

When the dal was dark enough, when Ashok's stirring had stilled, Mazumdar lowered him. The boy returned to his drawing. The pot simmered. The house filled with a smell that was not Wales.

The dal was ready.

V

Ruth did not ask again. After the café, after the *That's all right*, she did not return to the war. She built her understanding of her husband from the evidence available: the nightmares (infrequent, contained, the body stiffening beside her in the dark then releasing), the scars (a white line on his left hand, fourth metacarpal, she had asked about this once and he had said *an accident*), the habits, the plate-cleaning, the tidiness, the surgery door locked and checked twice, and the absences, the Bengali he did not speak, the India he did not visit, the family he mentioned only in the past tense.

She knew he had been a prisoner of war. She knew he had been at Colditz. She knew that what had happened there he would not discuss. What she could not have explained was when she had stopped wanting to know. There had been a time, early, before the boys, when she lay awake composing questions she would never ask. Then the questions stopped, and what replaced them was a conviction more practical than acceptance, the wall in the house was load-bearing, and you do not remove a load-bearing wall.

The silence was the weather of the marriage. They lived in it. The living was not unhappy. The living was ordinary, and the ordinariness was the achievement, a man who had stood before twenty German tanks with a handkerchief, coming home at six and eating his dinner and cleaning his plate and going to bed.

THE ARM

Chapter 28

I

The boy was six. His mother brought him in on a Tuesday afternoon, the afternoon surgery, two o'clock, the waiting room half-empty, the Welsh rain drawing lines on the window that the boy watched while his mother filled in the form.

Broken, the arm. Mazumdar knew this before the examination, the angle of the forearm, the boy's face white and drawn with the particular pallor of a child in pain. The mother held the boy close. Her eyes moved between Mazumdar's hands and his face, the brown hands on her son's white arm.

"Can you show me where it hurts?" The boy pointed, precisely, the body still honest before the mind learns to interpret. The break was in the distal radius. He could feel it through the skin, the discontinuity, the slight crepitus. He held the boy's arm gently, his fingers spanning the forearm, and the touch was still enough to make the boy flinch.

Plaster next. He wrapped the gauze stiffening as the plaster set, the boy watching his own arm disappear beneath the bandage. Mazumdar worked slowly, the layers even, the rhythm learned thirty years ago in Edinburgh and performed ten thousand times since, the same rhythm whether the patient was a child in Wales or a sepoy at Frontstalag 153. The hands did not distinguish.

"He'll need to keep it dry," he said. "Six weeks in the plaster. Bring him back in a fortnight."

A nod. She was already standing, already gathering the boy. At the door the boy looked back.

The door closed. He washed his hands. He stood at the basin and the water ran over his fingers, he watched it run and the watching lasted longer than the washing required.

I-A

Another patient. A farmer, Thomas Griffiths, sixty-three, the accent thick, the vowels of Welsh beneath English, the first language carried under the second the English like silt beneath a river's current. He came monthly. The blood pressure. The medication.

Mazumdar wrapped the cuff around the man's arm, the upper arm, the brachial artery beneath the skin, the stethoscope's diaphragm placed in the crook of the elbow. He inflated the cuff. The mercury rose. He listened, the first Korotkoff sound, the pulse appearing beneath the pressure, then the second, the third, the fourth, the fifth. Systolic: 158. Diastolic, 94. He released the valve. The mercury descended.

"Still high," he said. "Aye." "The tablets?"

"I take them." "Every day?" A pause. He did not take them every day. Mazumdar knew this pause. He had heard it ten thousand times. The pause was the body's negotiation with the mind, the mind preferring to believe the illness was optional, the body carrying the evidence that it was not.

He wrote the prescription. The pen's nib caught on the paper, the faintest resistance, the texture of the prescription pad rougher than the smooth letterhead he'd used in London. The handwriting that Ruth could barely read, the pharmacist decoded by familiarity rather than legibility. He tore the sheet and held it out.

"Mr Griffiths. The tablets are not optional." "Aye, Doctor." The man took the prescription. He folded it, carefully, the fold precise, the paper tucked into his shirt pocket. He stood. At the door he paused.

"My Annie says to tell you, the hip is better. Since the injection."

"Good." "She says you've got steady hands." The door closed. Mazumdar sat. The consulting room was quiet, the clock on the wall, the filing cabinet, the desk with its surface of green leather. He looked at his hands. The hands were on the desk. The fingers were long, the joints beginning to thicken, the first signs of the arthritis that would arrive fully in a decade. The hands were steady. They had always been steady. They had been steady holding a baton before twenty tanks, steady gripping the wire at Chartres, steady wrapping the gauze around a boy's broken arm. The steadiness was a fact about the hands. It was the only fact the patients needed.

He called the next patient. Mrs Evans. The knee. He rose from the chair and opened the door, patient after patient, year after year, the work a cast around him, firm, applied with precision, keeping the pressure where the pressure needed to be.

II

His hands hesitated for the first time in 1961.

A child, six years old, a cut on the forearm from a fall on gravel. Straightforward. Three sutures. He threaded the needle — the same motion he had performed ten thousand times since Edinburgh, the curved needle between thumb and forefinger, the thread approaching the eye. The thread did not enter. His fingers trembled at the eye of the needle. He steadied the right hand with the left. The thread entered. The suture proceeded. The suture was perfect. The child did not cry. The mother thanked him. He washed his hands. The water was cold. The soap was carbolic.

His knees began their protest in 1962. As a sediment, each day adding its layer, the accumulation invisible from above but felt in the body as weight. The surgery. The house. Ruth. The boys.

Bengali was thinning. He noticed it as a doctor notices the early signs of a disease. The language was still there. It surfaced in dreams. In counting — he still counted in Bengali, the numbers arriving in his mother's voice, *ek, dui, tin, char, panch,* and in moments of surprise or pain, when the body's first response preceded the mind's translation. Bengali had been there first, before the English, before the Latin, before the German. The base layer was eroding.

Reaching for a word one morning, *tulsi,* holy basil, and the reaching produced not the word but a gap, a space where the word should have been, the space shaped like the word but empty. He stood in the garden and looked at a plant that might have been tulsi, the mouth opened to speak the word and the mouth closed without the word arriving, the throat's contraction, the tongue's absence of purpose, the physical collapse of the capacity that had once been automatic as breathing. The not-knowing was the distance between Gaya and Wales measured in a single leaf, measured in the body's failure to name.

Ashok and Kamal learned ten Bengali words, at most between them. *Baba. Ma. Dal. Ruti. Jol.* The survival vocabulary. Mazumdar heard the words in his sons' English mouths, the sound of a language dying with the quiet inevitability of a river going underground.

A letter arrived from Calcutta. His cousin, the son of his father's brother, a man Mazumdar had not seen since 1939, had written in Bengali, the script careful, the ink blue, the paper thin enough to see the impression of the desk beneath it. Air mail. The stamp showed Nehru's face.

He sat at the kitchen table and read the letter. The paper was thin — airmail thin — and warm against his fingertips. The first paragraph was clear: news of the family, a death, an uncle, elderly, expected, the cousin's daughter's marriage. The second paragraph shifted into a register he recognised but could not follow, a literary Bengali, the sentences longer, the constructions ornate, the vocabulary of Tagore and Bankimchandra and the Calcutta periodicals. Mazumdar read the paragraph twice. He understood two-thirds of it, no more. The remaining third was a gap, not a wall but a thinning, the language present but insufficient, peripheral vision registering movement without detail.

Down went the letter. He picked it up again. The third paragraph asked whether he intended to visit. The question was direct, the cousin's directness, the man had always been blunt, and the directness required a direct answer, the answer was no and the no was a fact he did not examine because examination would have required a language for the examination in the language that was thinning.

He wrote his reply in English. He had not written Bengali in seven years. The pen hesitated above the paper, the hand knowing the shapes, the Bengali script still possible, the letters formed with the deliberation of a man copying rather than writing. He abandoned the attempt after two lines. The English reply was brief, correct, warm in its formality. He signed it in English. He posted it.

Ruth found the abandoned Bengali draft in the wastepaper basket. She smoothed it on the table, looked at the script: the loops, lines, diacritics of a language she could not read. She did not ask about it. She folded it and placed it in the drawer where she kept the letters from his family, the small archive of a country she had never visited, written in a script she had never learned, describing people she would never meet.

Dreams. Bengali surfaced in dreams like water through sand, unbidden, without grammar, the words arriving as sounds rather than meanings. He dreamed of his mother's voice calling him to eat, *Biren, khete esho,* and the calling was so precise that he could hear the specific note of her impatience, the second syllable of his name stressed because the calling had been repeated and the repetition carried its own emphasis. He woke in Devon. The room. Ruth breathing beside him. The voice was gone. The words remained for three seconds, held in the mouth, in the throat's muscle memory, and then they were gone too, and what remained was the shape of an absence, the negative space of a sound that had once been the first sound of every morning.

He counted in Bengali still. This was involuntary, the numbers arriving before the English, the sequence *ek, dui, tin, char, panch* preceding *one, two, three, four, five* by a fraction of a second. He counted his pulse in Bengali. He counted stitches in Bengali. He counted the steps from the consulting room to the front door in Bengali, fourteen, and the counting was the last outpost of a language that had once been as natural as breathing and was now a series of numbers, a child's vocabulary, a survival kit.

III

A Tuesday in 1965. Nothing happened. He saw fourteen patients. Mrs Thomas, the knee. Mr Davies, the chest. A child with an ear infection, the mother more anxious than the child. He wrote prescriptions, made notes, washed his hands between each patient the way he had washed them between cadavers in Edinburgh, the water cold, the soap carbolic. At lunch he ate a sandwich Ruth had made, ham and mustard, at his desk, the *Lancet* open beside the plate. The mustard was English mustard. He ate the sandwich. He saw six more patients. He drove home. He ate dinner. He cleaned the plate. He read the paper. He went to bed. Ruth's hand found his forearm. The day ended the way every day ended.

Bose grew larger. Not in his memory, in his memory Bose remained a man who drank coffee and spoke of his mother and removed his spectacles when he wanted to look at you. But outside his memory, Bose was becoming a god. *Netaji.* Portraits in millions of Indian homes. The mystery of his death sustaining him past mortality.

Jai Hind. Bose's greeting had become a national slogan. Mazumdar heard the words once on the radio, a broadcast from Delhi, and the hearing produced in his body a vibration, the words arriving from the space where the room in Berlin still existed.

IV

They moved to Essex. The practice was larger, the proximity to London offering anonymity, a place where a brown face in a consulting room was merely unusual rather than singular. The house was a Victorian semi with lime trees. The consulting room was at the front; the family lived at the back and above.

The boys went to school. Ashok came home one afternoon with a question he delivered in the tone of a child repeating something heard.

"Dad, where are you *really* from?" He said *India*. Kamal did not ask. Kamal watched. He had the watching quality, the clinical gaze, the observation that preceded speech.

THE SCREEN

Chapter 29

I

Pat Reid published *The Colditz Story* in 1952.

Mazumdar saw it in a bookshop window in Cardiff, the cover, the title, the photograph of a castle he recognised the way a man recognises his own handwriting. He stood on the pavement and looked at the book in the window and in those seconds the castle on the cover was not a photograph but a reconstruction in his body, the cobblestones in the courtyard, the iron rungs to the attic, the cold of the walls in February, the smell of cabbage from the kitchen, the scratch of wool against his neck. He could feel the castle in his hands.

He walked past the window. Behind him was a castle with a courtyard where a man had cooked curry for men who called him Jumbo. The cooking and the calling were the same captivity. The captivity was British, not German, and this was the distinction the book in the window would not make.

What the book would contain, he knew. He had known Pat Reid at Colditz. He had watched him plan and execute, had stood at the margins while Reid and the escape committee drew their maps and dug their tunnels. The book would be about escapes and camaraderie and British pluck. What the book would not contain, what no book about Colditz would ever contain, was the chair near the draught, the kitchen, the name *Jumbo*, the hands that scrubbed the mincemeat from the pot, the hunger strike that lasted sixteen days, the man who walked out of the front gate because the back routes were not available to him.

Airey Neave published *They Have Their Exits* in 1953. Mazumdar was not in it. P.R. Reid published a second volume in 1953. Mazumdar was not in that one either. The Colditz industry grew, and as it grew, the space it left for Mazumdar shrank, until the space was nothing, the same nothing he had occupied in the courtyard between 1941 and 1943, except that now the nothing was in print.

II

Television. The second erasure.

Colditz. BBC. 1972. The programme arrived in the living room in Essex on a Thursday evening, the castle broadcast into seventeen million homes, one of which was his.

Ruth watched. She had settled into her chair with a cup of tea and the *Radio Times* open on her lap. The word *Colditz* was in the listing and the word had thickened the room's silence into a different quality. She glanced at him. He had been reading the newspaper. He continued to read the newspaper.

Voices. English voices, the accents of the actors approximating the accents of the men he had known, the approximation close enough to trigger the memory and wrong enough to make the triggering painful. The casting did not include an Indian doctor who had lived in the same rooms and walked the same courtyard, eaten from the same kitchen and slept in the same attic.

He did not watch. He sat in the chair and read the newspaper.

Two series. Twenty-eight episodes. The board game came. The children's annual. The paperback tie-ins. Colditz became a word that English people used to mean *adventure* and that he heard the way you hear your own name mispronounced: recognisable, wrong, belonging to someone else.

A neighbour mentioned it. Harold Pennington, retired postman, the man who trimmed the hedge between their gardens with an annual precision that Mazumdar respected. Pennington was at the wall on a Saturday morning, the secateurs in his hand, the hedge between them.

"You were in the war, Dr Mazumdar?" "I was." "Colditz, wasn't it? Marvellous programme. Did you see it Thursday?"

"I did not." "Marvellous. The escapes. Tunnels, hidden rooms. You must have known some of those chaps."

"I knew some of them." "Extraordinary. Were you involved in the escaping?" Mazumdar looked at his neighbour. Pennington's face was open, interested, the face of a man for whom the war was a story with heroes, the heroes were English, and the story was entertainment. The face bore no malice. The ignorance was total and therefore blameless.

"I walked out through the front gate," Mazumdar said. Pennington laughed. The laughter was generous, he thought it was a joke. Mazumdar did not correct him. He returned to his weeding. Pennington returned to his hedge. The secateurs made their sound, a clean, metallic bite, and the hedge grew tidier and the conversation was over.

Ruth was in the kitchen. She had heard the exchange through the open window. She said nothing when he came in. She made tea. The tea arrived in his hands and the cup was warm and the warmth was sufficient.

The second series aired. More escapes. More tunnels. A love interest, a German woman, the narrative requiring a woman because television required a woman. He never watched the second series. The programme was in the house now, in the culture, in the conversations at the post office, in the *Radio Times* that Ruth left open on the arm of her chair. The castle was being reconstructed weekly in seventeen million living rooms and in none of them did a Bengali doctor stand in the kitchen cooking a curry that no one would eat.

In a shop window: the board game. *Escape from Colditz.* The castle rendered in bright colours on the box, the board showing tunnels and wire and guard towers. Players took turns rolling dice. The object was to escape. The game did not include a piece for the Indian doctor who could not escape because escape required the cooperation of men who would not cooperate with him, who had told the French he was a spy, who had assigned him the bunk in the attic and the seat near the draught, the mincemeat and the name *Jumbo*, a name he had carried through the castle as a dog carries what its owner gives it, without choice, without recourse.

The board game was priced at two pounds fifteen. He walked past.

At night, Ruth asleep, the house quiet, he stood in the dark sitting room and looked at the bookshelf. The Colditz books. Five of them now, their spines facing outward, the castle's name repeated in different fonts. He did not touch them. The shelf was at shoulder height. He could smell the books from here — paper and binding glue and the faint chemical of new print. He stood in the dark and the books were on the shelf, the shelf was in the room and the room was in the house and the house was in England and England was the country that had made him a soldier and made him a prisoner and made him a doctor and made him invisible.

He went to bed. Ruth's hand found his forearm. He slept. Ruth found a Colditz book in a shop. She bought it. She read it. She put it on the shelf. He saw it there daily, the spine, the title, the castle.

III

April the twentieth, 1968. A Saturday.

Enoch Powell stood before the cameras in Birmingham. *Rivers of Blood.* He did not say this, the phrase was the headline writer's, but it became the speech, the speech became a fact, the fact was that a senior British politician, someone who had served in the same army Mazumdar had served in, was standing before a crowd and saying that people who looked like Mazumdar should be sent home.

The radio was on. He was fifty-four. He had lived in Britain for thirty-seven years and had served in the British Army, had been starved and had escaped nine hundred kilometres and had kept his oath through everything the war and the silence and the years had asked of him. His hands were on the arms of the chair. The knuckles white. The masseter tightened — the quarter-millimetre, unchanged in twenty-four years, the metacarpophalangeals blanched from grip, the same hands that had held the handkerchief, that had scrubbed the pot, that had cut the wire at Chartres.

Ruth was in the kitchen. She heard the speech. She came to the doorway, a small woman, fair-haired, the hair greying at the temples, a tea towel in her hand that she twisted without noticing. She stood between the kitchen and the sitting room, her face changed in a way he saw and did not comment on. Then she said, very quietly, "That man." The two words hung in the room for a moment. She turned, went back to the kitchen and he heard the tap running, running longer than any washing-up required.

He listened to the entire speech. The listening was clinical, the same quality of attention he brought to a patient's description of symptoms, the careful auditing of language for the specific pathology it contained. Powell was an educated man, a classicist, a professor, a man who deployed words with the precision of a surgeon. Mazumdar recognised the technique. He had seen it in consultants who delivered terminal diagnoses with such fluency that the patient thanked them on the way out.

Bed. He did not discuss the speech with Ruth. They had discussed nothing that mattered since 1945. Yet the containing had a different quality now, because what was being contained was the present, what was happening to him in England. The oath had attached him to a country that did not want him. The oath still held. He was not leaving.

Dark. Ruth's breathing beside him. The house quiet, the boys asleep. He lay in the dark. The morning would come. He would rise, dress, go to the surgery. The patients would come and the patients would include people who had heard the speech and agreed with it and they would sit in his consulting room and show him their bodies and he would treat them.

The silence held.

IV

1971. Bangladesh.

The television again, Bengali faces, Bengali words in the mouths of reporters, Bengali bodies in the roads. The language dying in his mouth was the language being killed in the streets of Dhaka.

He watched the news every evening, the same chair, the same cup of tea. Ashok was nineteen. Kamal was seventeen. They were in the house. They knew their father was Indian but they did not know that the language being spoken on the screen was the language he dreamed in, that the refugees streaming across the border were walking roads he had walked as a boy.

Silence. Ruth brought more tea. The tea was English. The cup was English. The chair was English. The room was English. The man in the chair was not.

He went to bed. The television was turned off. The screen went dark, a rectangle of black glass reflecting the room, the chairs, the lamp, the Colditz book on the shelf. The boys went to school the next morning. The war lasted nine months. India intervened. Bangladesh was born. The language survived.

THE FOREARM

Chapter 30

I

Three in the morning. Devon.

He woke the way a doctor wakes — alert, heart rate elevated, the body transitioning from sleep to assessment in the time it takes a synapse to fire. The room. The curtains, heavy, drawn. The clock with its luminous hands, green, faintly radioactive, sufficient for the knowledge that the hour was three, the hour at which the body's temperature is lowest and the most people die.

Colditz. The washroom. The cold tap that ran brown water. The feel of the toothbrush in his hand, the bristles worn, the handle cracked. In the dream, the toothbrush was in his hand and the water was running, behind him a voice said *That bloody Mazumdar* and he did not turn around.

Dark. The Devon house made its night sounds, a pipe contracting, the boiler's quiet exhalation, a fox barking in the garden. The pillow was cool against the side of his face that had not been pressed against it. He turned into the cool — the specific temperature of cotton that has been exposed to night air while the body warms its other side. The house was their retirement house in Galmpton. The stairs creaked on the fourth step. The kitchen window didn't close properly. The garden wall held the day's warmth into the evening. He knew these things the way he had once known the castle, by the body's long habitation.

Ruth's hand found his forearm under the blanket. Cool palm against warm skin. She said nothing. He said nothing. They had done this a thousand times.

He breathed. The heart rate descended from eighty to seventy to sixty-four, his resting rate, the rate of a heart that had once descended to forty-two during the hunger strike and had never quite recovered, carrying a slight systolic murmur he had diagnosed himself and had not mentioned to Ruth.

He slept. Ruth's hand remained.

II

Negotiations had begun. He was seventy-eight. The arthritis had arrived in his hands, the hands, of course, and the joints stiffened overnight so that the first hour of each morning was a negotiation between the will and the cartilage.

The medical bag was in the hall cupboard. Leather, cracked along the spine where the wire at Chartres had scored it. He had not opened it in years. The bag was not retired. The bag was waiting.

His hearing was going. Not deafness but a thinning, the high registers fading first, the blackbird's song arriving simplified.

Gardening. The garden at Galmpton was small, a rectangle behind the house, bounded by stone walls on three sides, the fourth open to the Devon hills. The gate was iron, the hinge stiff, requiring the shoulder. On still mornings he could hear the sea. He grew vegetables. Tomatoes, beans, potatoes. He tended them with the same patient precision he had brought to the surgery.

He read medical journals, the advances in pharmacology and surgical technique described in language he could still follow though the practice was no longer his. He read them as a retired general reads dispatches from a front he no longer commands.

He did not read the Colditz books. They multiplied, a shelf in the Galmpton bookshop, a documentary on Channel 4. The castle had become a tourist attraction. Visitors bought postcards of the rooms where he had slept and cooked and starved himself for sixteen days.

III

Kamal came for dinner.

Down from London on a Saturday. The drive took three hours, the M4, the M5, the narrow Devon lanes where the hedgerows scraped the sides of the car. He came alone. His wife had stayed behind, work, the children. Kamal was forty-two, an accountant, a man of numbers, meticulous. He had his father's hands, the long fingers, the careful grip, and his father's quality of watching before speaking.

Ruth had been cooking since morning. The shepherd's pie was her discipline, the lamb minced, the onion soft, the potato piped in ridges across the top. She had made it for forty years and the recipe had not changed because the recipe was the marriage: reliable, warm, unquestioned. She had also baked, a Victoria sponge, the jam homemade, the cream from the farm at the end of the lane. The sponge had a weight in the hand when he helped carry it to the table, the weight of eggs and flour and sugar, warm at the centre.

The table was set for three. Ruth's table, the cloth white, the cutlery aligned. She had placed flowers in a vase, daffodils from the garden, the stems cut at an angle because Mazumdar had once told her, thirty years ago, that angled cuts allowed better water uptake, and she had remembered this as she remembered everything he had said about the body's workings, with precision, without comment.

Kamal arrived at six. He kissed Ruth at the door, bending to her, the height differential requiring the bend, Ruth's hand on his arm. He shook his father's hand. The handshake was brief, formal, the formality a habit between two men who had never learned another gesture. Mazumdar noted his son's grip. Firm. The metacarpals in good alignment. No tremor.

They sat. The shepherd's pie arrived. Ruth carrying it from the kitchen in the dish she had used since Wales, the ceramic heavy, the heat requiring oven gloves. She served. Mazumdar ate. He cleaned the plate, the fork moving across the surface, gathering, the plate's surface visible beneath the gathering, and then the bread, torn, the bread's interior surface wiping the china until the china was white.

Kamal watched the wiping. He had watched it all his life, the methodical clearing, the bread used as an instrument. He did not know why his father ate this way. He had theories: wartime rationing, Indian custom, simple habit. The theories were not wrong. They were insufficient.

They talked. Kamal's work, the firm had expanded, new clients, a move to larger offices. The children, Rohan was ten and doing well at school, Priti was seven and had started violin. Ruth told a story about the cat getting into the surgery, "I found him in the filing cabinet, Biren, sitting on the Ps", and Mazumdar laughed, the rare short laugh that his sons had learned to value for its scarcity.

Ruth cleared the plates. She brought the sponge. She cut it with the knife held vertical, the slices even, her precision in this domestic geometry as consistent as Mazumdar's in his surgical geometry, the two precisions having lived alongside each other for forty years, neither commenting on the other.

Kamal ate the sponge. He complimented Ruth. He drank the tea she brought. He sat in the chair and the chair was the same chair, the room the same room, the window the same window, and outside the Devon dark had settled and the garden was invisible.

Then Kamal asked. He did not build to it. He put his fork down. He looked across the table. The looking was direct. Mazumdar recognised it. It was the look he had trained on patients for forty years, the look that said *I am going to ask you now and the asking will be specific.*

"Dad, what actually happened to you during the war?" Mazumdar's hands stopped moving. The fork rested on the plate. The plate was clean, already clean, the bread having done its work.

Two seconds. Three. In those three seconds the room contained everything, the tanks on the road, the handkerchief, the castle, the man across the table in Berlin, the sixteen days, the wire in the dark, Singh's voice saying *Shabash*, the corridor in the War Office, fifty years.

Ruth was at the end of the table. Her hands were in her lap. She had been waiting for this question for forty-six years. Her body was still, the stillness of a woman who has rehearsed a moment so many times that the moment's arrival produces a settling, a finally.

"A long time ago," he said. "Not worth going into." Fork up. He resumed eating. The fork moved to the sponge. The sponge was on his plate and the fork cut into it and the cutting was a completion, the conversation over, the door closed, the lock turned.

"There's more pie if anyone wants it," Ruth said. "The crust came out better this time."

Her voice was steady. The offer was ordinary, a woman offering food, a table with three people, a Saturday in Devon. Beneath the offer, the knowledge that the door had closed again and that she would not force it. She had never forced it. Forty-three years of not-forcing was its own kind of discipline, its own endurance, its own held breath.

Kamal looked at his mother. He looked at his father. He looked at the fork in his father's hand, the fork steady, the hand steady, the man behind the hand as unreachable as he had been at every dinner for forty-six years.

He did not ask again. He helped clear the table. He kissed Ruth at the door and shook his father's hand, briefly, firmly, holding it a moment longer than usual before letting go. He drove back to London in the dark.

Mazumdar stood at the kitchen door. The lane was empty. The sound of Kamal's engine faded, through the hedgerows, past the farm, toward the main road, and then the sound was gone and what remained was Devon. The hedge. The stars, sparse, the cloud cover from the west. A fox moved in the garden and stopped, looked at the lit doorway and moved on.

Ruth was behind him. He could hear her at the sink, the tap running, the plates, the small percussion of a kitchen being put to rights. Then the sounds stopped. She was standing at the sink, holding a plate, not washing it. He did not turn around. She did not speak. The kitchen held them separately, him at the door, her at the sink, the table cleared between them, the cloth still damp where she had wiped it.

He closed the door. He checked the lock.

Dark. Bed. The Devon house settled around them, the pipe, the boiler, the fox again, distant. Ruth's hand found his forearm under the blanket. Cool palm against warm skin. The same gesture. The same forearm. The evening had asked everything and received nothing and the gesture did not change. They had done this a thousand times. They would do it again.

THE TAPE

Chapter 31

I

March. A letter arrived.

It was on the mat with the other post, a gas bill, a circular from the church, a letter from the medical council. The letter was typed. The envelope was institutional, the paper heavier than personal stationery, the stamp franked by a machine.

Imperial War Museum. London. He held the envelope without opening it for ten seconds.

He opened it. A researcher was compiling oral histories of prisoners of war. Mazumdar's name had been found in an archive, a Red Cross document, a repatriation record, a line in a book about Colditz. He would never know which line, in which book, because the books did not contain him except as a footnote.

Would he be willing to speak? Letter on the kitchen table. Tea made. He drank the tea standing at the window, watching the garden, the March garden, not yet in leaf, the soil dark from winter rain. Ruth was upstairs. He could hear her, the tap, the cupboard, the small domestic percussion.

He did not know why he said yes. He picked up the telephone. He dialled the number on the letter. A voice answered, young, professional, and the voice asked if he was willing, he said yes and it was the first word he had spoken about the war in fifty years.

II

He did not tell Ruth.

This was not a decision. It was a continuation, the silence so thoroughly embedded in the marriage that even its breaking was conducted within it. He made the arrangements by telephone when she was out. He prepared, with the slow internal reorganisation of fifty years' weight about to be set down.

In the consulting room, where patients had once sat and told him their bodies' secrets. The room still smelled faintly of carbolic. The shelves held the medical journals, the books, the instruments wrapped in cloth. He sat in the chair that had been the patient's chair. The researcher sat in his.

He spoke. May 1940. The words came first, dates, places, facts, the mind ordering them as it had ordered everything for fifty years, by function, by precision, by the refusal to look at what the ordering concealed.

His hand gripped the microphone. A small red light on the device. His fingers felt the weight of it, unexpected, requiring a grip, the grip requiring his attention, surgery's attention, the hand's old precision, the hand remembering its training, the holding precise. The researcher sat in his chair, the surgeon's chair, young, patient, a face unmarked by what a face learns when it listens to a man speak about what speech had cost. Mazumdar looked at the device. The small red light. He opened his mouth.

May 1940. Not "I was captured." Not "I remember." The clinical mind does not begin with the self. It begins with the date. The convoy. The tanks. The sound of the shells, a compression, the air folding inward. He spoke these things with the precision he had learned in Edinburgh, the precision that had held him through the years in the castle, the precision that had allowed the body to function while the mind observed the body functioning. The dates arrived without tremor. The places named. The facts, five hundred men, three burning ambulances, the helmet left in the road, each fact a small stone placed in a structure that could be examined because it was not him.

But at sixteen days the voice changed. Not visibly. The researcher would not have noted it. The pauses came. From the remembering too much at once, the hunger strike, the pulse at forty-two, Ferguson's face on day fourteen, nothing, never mind, the face giving no sign, the body as an instrument and the instrument as the measure, and the measuring voice fracturing because what it measured could not be measured in words. His hands gripped the chair arms. The knuckles whitened. He could see this, the doctor watching the doctor watching the body respond to what the body was being asked to recall. The microphone held what the hands could not contain. In the room, Mazumdar and the recorder and the young researcher and the space where the clinical voice had been and where a different voice now was, not the inventory voice, not the diagnostic voice, but the voice beneath both, the voice the fifty years of not-speaking had not erased.

The pause held. Ruth, beyond the door, heard it, not what was being said but the sound of the saying reaching its limit. The silence in the room. Then the voice resumed. Different. Not the inventory voice. The voice of a man inside the moment. The voice naming things that could not be named. Bose. The coffee. The sound of Bengali on a platform. The thing he had refused. Words, but beneath the words a current that ran too deep for the microphone to record, too deep for the researcher to fully hear, too deep for any listening after this to completely reach.

His hands remained on the arms of the chair. The wood knew his grip. The gripping was all that held it, the voice, the words, the facts, the memory: together in the room with the red light, with the young face, with the door between him and Ruth, with the silence that had held for fifty years and that was now, for the first time in fifty years, being asked to speak.

The session lasted hours. He did not tell them about the Crack. He did not tell them about the precise quality of Ferguson's silence on day fourteen. He did not tell them about the taste of Bose's coffee, the first real coffee in three years, and the drinking of it had been the most dangerous act of the evening because the coffee was an intimacy and the intimacy was Bose's weapon and the weapon was more effective than any argument. He did not tell them about the sound of Bengali heard across a station platform in Berlin, and what that sound had opened in his chest, and why it could not be closed again.

III

Ruth heard fragments. Not the words themselves, they arrived muffled, pressed through plaster and lathe. *Colditz. Bose.* A name repeating twice, the emphasis softening on the second occurrence, the way a man's voice abandons precision when it moves toward what lives beneath speech.

He was in the consulting room. The door was closed. She did not open it.

She moved instead into the kitchen, the space where she had sorted his mail for forty-six years, made the tea he drank standing at the window, arranged the plates in patterns only she understood. The kettle was there on the stove. She filled it from the tap and set it on the flame. The water took time. The water always took time, and she had learned long ago, in their first flat in Edinburgh, when he was still speaking, that the waiting between filling and boiling was a space where thinking stopped and presence took its place. The watching. The simply being present in the room while the small physics of heating occurred.

The kettle began to climb. She did not leave. She stood. The whistle approached, a small rising note that was the same whistle every afternoon, yet sounded each time as though arriving for the first time. From the consulting room, the murmur continued. His voice at a distance. A pause. The researcher's voice. Another pause.

She made two cups. One for him, the white one without the hairline fracture, the one she kept for him, and one she would place outside the door. The tea steeped. The colour moved from nothing through amber to a brown she had learned to read the way her husband read X-rays — by the density of what the light passed through. Forty-six years of this. She did not know the duration. She simply knew when it was ready.

The cup for outside the door, this one she held for a moment after pouring. Her hands were in view of nothing, no one. Her fingers curved around the ceramic. It was warm. The heat itself was a information, the temperature, the current, the fact that something hot could be carried and held. She had twisted the tea towel before setting the cup down, a gesture from the marriage so old it had become unconscious, the wringing motion, the releasing, the twisting again, the same motion she had performed on cold mornings in their first year when she was waiting for him to emerge from the study, the waiting becoming itself a kind of presence, a kind of standing-guard, a kind of love that had no name in their vocabulary and so required no speech.

She set the cup outside the consulting room door. Ceramic on wood. The small click of contact. She did not wait. She turned. Her gait returning to the kitchen was slower than usual. Not fatigue — he knew fatigue's rhythm.

He was still speaking. Her hand found his forearm. She held it for a long time. Then she stood, collected the researcher's cup, carried it to the kitchen, washed it, dried it, placed it on the shelf with the others.

IV

The tapes existed in the house.

Small cassettes in a drawer in the consulting room, the magnetic ribbon holding his voice the way the silence had held his story. Ruth did not play them. She knew they were there. The tapes were sealed with an embargo, the recordings to be released only after his death.

She would hear them eventually. Decades later, long after his death in December 1997, a historian would come. A man with a notebook and the cassettes. He would sit in the kitchen, play the tapes. Ruth would hear her husband's voice for the first time since the last morning, speaking about things she had slept beside for forty-six years.

We were both in floods by the end. But that was later. For now, for March 1996, for the kitchen and the dal and the bread, the silence held. Not the old silence. A new silence. The silence of a man who has spoken and a woman who has heard fragments and neither of them knows what the other knows.

The silence held.

SECTION III

STILL

THE GARDEN

Chapter 32

I

April. The garden needed turning.

At the kitchen door he stood and looked at it, the rectangle of soil behind the house, bounded by stone walls, the fourth side open to the Devon hills where the morning mist was still sitting in the valleys like milk poured and not yet absorbed. The garden had wintered badly. The frost had taken the rosemary and cracked the terracotta pot by the wall and the soil had the compacted, ungenerous look of ground that has been cold for too long. He could see what needed doing. He had always been able to see what needed doing. The seeing and the doing were separating now, and the gap was his body, eighty-two years old, opinionated about kneeling.

He put on his boots at the kitchen door. Green Wellington boots, cracked at the ankles, the rubber perished in places. He pulled them on standing, one hand against the doorframe for balance. He had not needed the doorframe last spring. The needing was new and he noted it precisely, without commentary, the way a doctor reads a chart.

Ruth was in the kitchen behind him. He could hear her, the tap, the kettle filling, the quiet chime of cups lifted from the shelf. These sounds were the morning. They had been the morning for twenty years in this house, for twenty years before that in Essex, for the years before Essex in Wales, the geography changing and the sounds remaining.

He stepped into the garden. The air was cold, April cold, Devon cold. The grass was wet. His boots left dark prints on the lawn where the dew was displaced. He crossed to the far wall where the tools hung on nails. The fork. The spade. The trowel, its handle smooth from years of his grip, the wood darkened where his palm had polished it. He took the fork.

A robin was on the wall. It watched him with the black-eyed directness of a bird that has decided a man with a fork is a man who will produce worms. Ruth had taught him the birds, robin, wren, blue tit, great tit, a man from the plains of Bihar acquiring the vocabulary of a Devon garden in his sixties. The fork handle was smooth where his grip had worn it. Ash wood. The grain under his thumb, the warmth of the handle — wood holds the heat of the hand that holds it. He drove the fork into the soil. Through the kitchen window behind him, the glass framed a rectangle of sky — and for a half-second the rectangle was the courtyard's, grey, Saxon, twenty-seven metres on three sides. Then Devon returned. The soil resisted, the winter had hardened it. The driving required more effort than it should have, the effort in his shoulders, his lower back, his wrists, which had begun their morning protest. He turned the fork. A clod of earth broke and the breaking released a smell, dark, mineral, alive, the smell that rose was dark and sweet and cold, the smell of earth that has been turned.

The morning continued.

The sea was audible. A mile and a half to the east, the estuary where the Dart met the Channel. On still mornings the sound carried, a kind of breathing, the coast's pulse beneath the birdsong. He had chosen this house partly for the sea. He had not said this to Ruth. The sea was a sound he needed in the mornings, the sound of water that was not underground.

An hour's work. The fork turned the beds along the south wall, the tomato beds, the soil breaking into smaller pieces, the worms exposed and recoiling. His back reported first. Then his hands. The tremor in his right hand had arrived on schedule, a fine vibration he could suppress by gripping but not by willing, the will and the tremor running on different circuits. He set the fork against the wall. He straightened. The straightening took longer than it once had.

Ruth appeared at the kitchen door with tea. She held two cups and crossed the garden with the careful steps of a woman walking on uneven ground in house shoes. She had not changed into outdoor shoes to bring him tea. That was Ruth. She held the cups carefully, with an attentiveness to how the liquid rested inside, how the weight distributed, her wrists bearing the load. The warmth rose from the cups into her palms, and she had not poured more than he could drink.

Her pupils were slightly dilated. Not the light — the kitchen had been brighter. The dilation was adrenaline's residue. She had been standing at the kitchen window watching him work and the watching had cost her something.

"Biren." She said his name. She said it the way she had begun saying it since the recording, with an attention that had not been there before, as though the name now contained more than it had contained. The utterance itself was a form of care.

He took the cup. Their fingers touched on the ceramic. The touch was cooler than it should have been, her hands were cold from the morning air. The blood vessels in her fingers were constricted, the capillaries conserving the body's core heat. He registered this without wanting to, the medical observation, automatic. But beneath the observation was the fact of her cold hand holding a hot cup, the hand continuing to hold despite the cold, continuing for him. The recording was in a drawer in the consulting room. The drawer was closed.

They stood in the garden and drank their tea. The mist was lifting from the valleys. A blackbird was singing from the wall, the song simplified, the high notes absent, the hearing thinning in the frequencies the blackbird needed most.

"The rosemary's gone," he said. "I know. I'll get another from the garden centre." "The pot's cracked too." "I saw." They stood in the garden. The tea cooled in their hands.

II

She watched him now. He knew this because he had spent sixty years being watched, by guards, by prisoners, by patients, by the stares on the pavements of Cardiff. Ruth's watching was different. Her eyes stayed on him a moment longer when he dressed, with the attention of a woman cataloguing the man who shared the house, marking the changes. Her gaze followed his hands across the breakfast table. She looked at him as relatives look at patients after a diagnosis, but relatives also look at people they love with the same intensity, and he was not certain where the looking fell, whether it landed in concern or in a feeling she could not name.

She did not ask. She said: "More tea?" She said: "The post's come." She said: "Biren, your glasses are on the shelf."

Biren. The name again. His name in her mouth, carrying new freight. The weight of the recording, the weight of what she had heard through the plaster, the weight of forty-six years held in a single utterance.

III

Once, she was looking at his chest.

Not staring. Ruth did not stare. A glance that lasted two seconds longer than a glance should last, the eyes finding a place on his body and remaining there with an attention he could not immediately classify.

He was changing his shirt. The garden had dirtied the one he was wearing and he had come inside, unbuttoned it and pulled it off and was reaching for the clean shirt on the chair when her eyes found the place. The place was on his chest. Left side. A line — pale, slightly raised, running diagonally from the left shoulder toward the right hip. The line where the sacred thread had rested for fifteen years, from the Upanayana ceremony in Gaya when he was eleven to the delousing room at Kassel when he was twenty-six, the cotton thread worn against the skin day and night, the body carrying the mark of the thing long after the thing was gone.

He had not looked at the line in years. It was there the way scars are there: part of the body's surface, carrying its history in the tissue without announcing it. A dermatologist would have classified it as a pressure mark. A priest would have classified it differently.

Ruth's eyes were on the line. Two seconds. Then she looked away. She picked up the dirty shirt. She said nothing. She carried the shirt to the laundry basket and he heard the lid open and close.

He put on the clean shirt. He buttoned it. The line disappeared beneath the cotton. The sacred thread was in Kassel. He did not know where it was. The thread was gone. The line remained. Ruth had seen the line and had said nothing.

He went to the kitchen. She was at the sink. He sat in his chair. She brought his tea. He opened the newspaper. Outside, the garden waited. The turned soil in the south beds was dark and open and ready for planting. The cracked pot sat against the wall. The stone walls held the morning light.

Newspaper. Ruth moved in the kitchen behind him, the sounds of her morning, the tap and the cupboard. He turned the page. The sound of an ordinary morning, and the ordinary morning was what remained after everything else had been spent.

THE TOAST

Chapter 33

I

Months passed. The way months pass when the body has entered the pace of seasons, the garden marking time better than the calendar, the tomatoes arriving in July and the runner beans in August and the dahlias in September, each arrival a measurement the body understood, the body had planted them, the body's calendar.

Thinner. Not dramatically — the quiet thinning of a body that has begun to spend more than it takes in, the metabolism's long decline, the muscles losing their argument with gravity. His trousers needed a belt he had not needed a year ago. His shirts sat differently on his shoulders. Ruth noticed, she noticed everything, she had spent forty-six years noticing, and she increased the portions without comment, as you increase the draught on a fire that is cooling, an act of will she performed with the same quiet stubbornness she had brought to everything since the bank counter in Cardiff.

Less cooking now. The dal, his mother's recipe, the spices weighed in his palm, he still made on Sundays, but the standing at the stove tired him in a way it had not tired him a year ago, and the tiredness was in his legs, his back and the small bones of his feet, which had never fully recovered from the march. From Étaples to Nijmegen. The same feet in a kitchen in Devon fifty-six years later, becoming harder now.

Hands. The arthritis had deepened over the winter. The metacarpophalangeal joints, the joints were swollen, the fingers stiff in the mornings, the grip weaker. He could no longer open jars. This bothered him more than the walking or the hearing or the tremor, the jars were small, specific, and the specificity was what held him. A surgeon who cannot open a jar. The diagnosis was osteoarthritis, progressive, bilateral. The treatment was paracetamol and patience. The patience was harder than the paracetamol.

Ruth opened the jars. She did this without being asked, the prescriptions transcribed, the appointments kept, the dosages corrected. She had done everything in the marriage without being asked. She opened the jar and placed it on the counter and he took what he needed, her hand steadying the jar, his hand reaching, the coordination of decades. Collaboration so practised it had become invisible, except that it was not invisible. The watching had shown him, the way she held the jar, her wrist rotating, her hand remaining steady, the small strength of that action. Not strength. Precision. Twenty years in this kitchen, thirty before that, the repetition lodged in the muscles themselves.

Ruth's hands drew his attention. He had trained himself to look at hands, the hands of professors in Edinburgh, the hands of patients, the hands of nurses and soldiers. He looked at her hands, and what he saw was the action itself, the grip, the twist, the placement on the counter. She did not look like a woman with swollen knuckles. She looked like a woman opening a jar. The hands, seventy-four years old, the skin thin, the veins visible, were simply doing what hands do. Here. Back to the newspaper.

II

October. A morning.

Early, the waking, by the body's habit, the internal clock that had run since the camps and that woke him at six regardless of season or need. The room was dark. The curtains held out the Devon dawn, which in October arrived late and grey, the light reluctant, the sky giving only what it had to. Ruth's breathing beside him. Steady. The rhythm unchanged in forty-six years, she slept on her left side, facing him, her breath a tide he had learned to match his own to without knowing he was matching it.

Stillness. Not the stillness of a man at rest. It was the stillness of a man listening, to the house, to his body, to an October morning in Devon when the first frost has come and the garden has entered its dormancy, the air through the window's imperfect seal carries the smell of cold soil and fallen leaves and the faint salt of the estuary.

The heart. He listened to it each morning, with the body's own attention, the internal ear that a doctor develops over decades, the ear that can hear a murmur without instruments. The murmur was there. Systolic, grade two, the same murmur he had diagnosed himself years ago and had not mentioned to anyone. It was his murmur. It belonged to the same heart that had descended to forty-two beats per minute on a bunk in Colditz and had never quite forgiven him.

Rising was a process now — a sequence: turn, sit, pause, stand. The pause was where the body negotiated. The knees.

The back. The ankles that stiffened overnight and required thirty seconds of weight-bearing before they would consent to walking. He stood at the bedside and the standing was an agreement between his will and his joints, temporary, renewable each morning, subject to revision.

The bathroom. The tap ran hot then cold then hot, the pipes protesting the distance from the boiler. He waited for the warmth. The shaving. The face in the mirror — thinner than last year, the cheekbones more prominent, the temporal wasting he had once diagnosed in others now present in his own reflection. He shaved with care. The razor moved over terrain he knew intimately, the jaw, the chin, the upper lip, the hollow beneath the cheekbone where the blade must be angled precisely. He had shaved this face for sixty years. The face had changed and the shaving had not.

Shirt, trousers, cardigan. No tie. The retirement had ended the ties, the one concession to informality that he permitted himself. Buttoned. He checked his appearance in the mirror, the checking automatic, the posture straight, the shoulders back. The straightness had been the man since the recruiting office in London in 1939.

Kitchen. Cold, the kitchen. The heating had not come on. The timer was set for seven and it was six-fifteen and the house was still in its overnight state, the tiles cold beneath his slippers, the window dark, the garden invisible beyond the glass. He filled the kettle. He put it on. He took the bread from the bin. A white loaf, sliced, the slices uniform. The bread was English bread, soft and without crust to speak of. Nothing like his mother's kitchen, nothing like the French farmhouses, nothing like the dense dark bread of the German camps — the bread of a life lived in England for sixty years.

Two slices in the toaster. The toaster was old — chrome, the kind with a lever that pressed down with a mechanical resistance, the bread descending into the element's glow. He pressed the lever. The bread descended. He waited.

The kettle began its sound, the low hum building to a rumble, the water's protest against the element, the sound filling the kitchen as presence. He made tea. The teabag in the cup, not loose tea — not the tea of Gaya or the tea of the café in Cardiff where Ruth had said *That's all right*, but a teabag in a mug, the efficiency of a country that had streamlined its rituals without noticing what the streamlining cost. He poured the water. The steam rose.

The toast arrived. The lever released with a metallic sound. The bread rose, browned, transformed by heat from soft into sharp. He took it, placed it on a plate. The butter was in the dish on the counter.

Buttering the toast, his movements precise. The knife — a butter knife, broad, blunt, the same knife they had used for twenty years in this kitchen — moved across the surface of the bread. The butter spread. The hands were steady, or nearly steady, the tremor suppressed by the grip, the grip sufficient for this, for toast, for the act the morning required.

The bread. Toast, this morning. Two slices, browned, the butter melting into the surface. Ruth had cut the toast diagonally, she always cut diagonally, the geometry of forty-six years, and the triangles sat on the plate, the plate sat on the table and the table was English oak. He ate. The toast was warm. The butter was salted. The crumbs fell onto the plate and he gathered them with his fingertip, each crumb, each fragment. Ruth watched this over her own cup. She had watched it for forty-six years. She did not know that the gathering was a reflex trained by sixteen days without food, that the body never forgets its hunger.

Bread, not rice. The morning's carbohydrate arrived in the wrong grain and had arrived in the wrong grain for fifty years and the wrongness had become rightness by duration, by repetition, by the slow replacement of one life with another.

Plate to the table. He sat. The chair received him. The newspaper was on the table where Ruth had left it the night before. He unfolded it. He folded it into quarters. He began to read.

Ruth came in. She was in her dressing gown, the blue one, the terrycloth worn thin at the elbows, the belt tied loosely. Her hair was uncombed. Her feet were in slippers that made a soft sound on the tiles, a shuffling, the sound of a woman who had not yet fully committed to the vertical. She filled the kettle again. She made her own tea. She made toast. She sat across from him at the table.

Her right wrist rotated as she set the cup down, the pronation slightly guarded, the ulnar deviation more pronounced than it had been a year ago. The metacarpophalangeal joints were thickening, the early nodal changes at the distal interphalangeals. She held the cup with both hands now. She had not needed both hands a year ago.

"Morning." "Morning." It had been the same exchange for forty-six years. Every piece, every crumb. He ate his toast completely. He used the crust to wipe the last trace of butter from the plate, the bread moving in a circular motion, the plate cleaned, the china showing through. He had done this every morning since the camps. The cleaning was not a decision. It was discipline, the same discipline that dressed and buttoned and folded, the body's insistence that nothing be wasted, the body remembered what happened when there was nothing.

Ruth was watching. He could feel it without looking up, her eyes on his hands, on the plate, on the circular motion of the bread. The watching had a quality he could not read. He did not try to read it. He cleaned the plate and set down the crust and picked up the newspaper.

The mornings accumulated. May, June, July. Each morning the same morning: the kettle, the toast, the newspaper, Ruth across the table, the exchange ("Morning." "Morning.") and the eating and the silence between the eating and the reading, furnished with decades of proximity, a room whose objects had been placed so long ago that no one remembers placing them.

The garden grew. He planted the tomatoes in May, the seedlings thin and pale from the greenhouse, the planting requiring kneeling, the kneeling requiring the consent of the knees, and the knees consented with conditions. He planted the runner beans against the south wall. The dahlias. The courgettes that Ruth had not asked for and would not refuse. The planting was a calendar and the calendar was his, and the tending was a practice he could still perform, the body still capable of this, the bending, the digging, the patient daily inspection of what the soil was doing.

In July the tomatoes ripened. He brought them in, three, four at a time, warm from the vine, the skin taut, the smell green and sharp on his fingers. He placed them on the kitchen windowsill where the light caught them and the red deepened over days. Ruth sliced them for salads. He ate the salads. He ate everything.

Ashok came in August. Their older son drove down from London on a Saturday, the car in the lane, the door, the sound of a man's shoes on the gravel path, and Mazumdar stood at the kitchen window, watched his son walk toward the house and the watching held the boy's gait inside it, unchanged beneath the decades, still there inside the man.

Ashok was forty-four. His hair greyed at the temples. He wore a shirt without a tie, the informality of a generation that did not understand dressing as architecture. His face was Ruth's face, the jaw, the eyes. His voice was English. The accent of Essex schools, English life. No Bengali. The language had never been given. The language his father carried underground, the language that surfaced in dreams and in the recording, the son had never received it.

They had lunch. Ruth cooked. Ashok talked: about work, about his children, about a holiday he was planning. The talking was easy, the ease of children who do not know their parents, the surface bright, the depth unvisited. Mazumdar listened. He ate his soup. He cleaned his bowl.

"Dad." Ashok paused. The pause held weight. "Are you all right? Mum said you've been, she said you made some recordings."

"For the Imperial War Museum." "About the war." "Yes." Ashok waited. Ashok's waiting. He had been told, all his life, that his father was in the war. Who has accepted the telling as complete. Who is now, at forty-four, sensing that the telling was not complete and that the thing not told is large.

"Would you — can I hear them?" "They're embargoed. After I'm gone." "After you're —" "After I'm gone, Ashok. That's the arrangement." The sentence closed the door. Mazumdar could feel it close, the same mechanism that had closed doors in the colonel's office at Colditz and in the consulting room in Wales and in every room where the silence had been tested. The mechanism worked. The door closed. Ashok nodded, the nod slow, and returned to his soup. Ruth was at the sink. Her back was to them. The tap was running. The tap ran longer than it needed to.

Ashok left on Sunday. He stood at the car and held Mazumdar's hand, a handshake that lasted a moment longer than handshakes last, the grip firm, the son's hand large and warm around the father's thinner hand. Then the car, the lane, the sound diminishing, and

Mazumdar stood at the kitchen door and watched the lane after the car was gone.

Kamal came the following weekend. He drove down from London, the same drive, the M4, the M5, the Devon lanes. He sat in the kitchen with Ruth and talked about the children, the garden, the weather, and the talking was warm and the warmth was real and the real was the surface and beneath the surface the river ran, the same river that ran beneath every conversation in this house, the question that had been asked once, in this kitchen, on a Saturday evening, and had not been answered, and the not-answering had become a fact of the family, not a wound but a weather, the way the silence between Mazumdar and Ruth was a weather, the way the silence between Mazumdar and everything he had been before the war was a weather. Both sons knew their father. Neither son knew what their father had been. The Phalgu ran where no one could see it. The cracked earth of the dry bed was clean, unmarked. The surface was dust, but beneath the dust the water moved, patient, invisible, the way a river moves when it has learned to move in the dark.

In the consulting room, the small room at the back of the house that had been his study since they moved to Devon, a tape recorder sat on the desk. Not the IWM's machine. His own. A small cassette recorder he had bought at the electronics shop in Paignton, the purchase unremarked, the machine carried home in a plastic bag and placed on the desk beside the lamp, the medical journals and the photograph of his parents. The machine sat there. He had not used it. He had not pressed the record button or spoken into it or decided what he would say if he did. The machine was there: present, unused, the possibility of speech held in the mechanism the way a seed holds the possibility of a plant, dormant, waiting for conditions the soil had not yet provided.

He did not know who the machine was for. Not the IWM, they had their recordings. Not Ruth, Ruth had heard fragments, and the fragments were what the fragments were. For Ashok? For Kamal? For the sons who had grown up above the underground river and had never been told the river was there? He did not know. The machine was not used. He was not certain the speaking had accomplished what the speaking was meant to accomplish. He was not certain what the speaking was meant to accomplish. The afternoons passed: the consulting room, the medical journals, the lamp, the photograph, the recorder. The silence held.

THE MEMORY

Chapter 34

I

In the garden was where the memory came.

He was outside — late morning, the sun thin and pale, the October light making everything look as though it had been painted with a single wash. He was sitting on the bench by the south wall. He had been turning the compost, the last garden task of the season, the fork driven into the dark mass of vegetable matter and leaf mould and grass cuttings, the turning releasing steam and the smell of decomposition, which was also the smell of renewal, the one process containing both. His back had stopped him after twenty minutes. He sat on the bench, negotiation, the body's terms accepted, the fork resting against the wall.

Visible now, the Devon hills. The mist had burned off and the Devon hills rolled south toward the coast, gentle, green, nothing like the flat plains of Bihar and nothing like the grey hills of Saxony visible from the courtyard at Colditz and nothing like the dark fields of France through which he had run with Singh. The hills were Devon hills and they rolled in the Devon way, he sat on a bench in his garden and watched them, an ordinary act on an ordinary morning in October.

Without announcement, the memory. It arrived without announcement, simply present. Gaya. The platform. The heat of a Bihar morning pressing against his uniform. The smell of samosas frying and chai boiling, coal smoke and the particular smell of an Indian railway platform that is like no other smell because it contains food and fuel and humanity and dust in a combination that the nose receives as a single thing, and the single thing is India.

He was walking back along the platform with the samosas. The oil staining through the newspaper. The chai in clay cups in his other hand. Bhola's family in the compartment. He was walking with the stride of a British officer, straight-backed, measured, the pace of rank.

The sergeant major was already there when he saw him. He remembered this. The sergeant already in the corridor of the compartment, already the obstacle, the man's back to him, the bulk of the man filling the corridor with the authority of obeying and giving orders in the same hour and cannot distinguish between the two.

What he remembered was the sergeant's face when the sergeant turned. Not surprise, the memory did not give him surprise. The memory gave him a different gift. The sergeant's face was set, deliberate. The expression of knowing what he was doing and was doing it because he could and because the people he was doing it to were people it could be done to. The contempt was in the jaw. The jaw was set, the mind behind it having made a decision and the decision was that the person in front did not matter.

"Stand to attention." He heard his own voice. The voice was not the voice of the recording — not the slightly hoarse voice of an eighty-two-year-old man speaking into a machine in Devon. The voice was the voice of the platform. Young. Sharp. The voice of a man who had carried the oath for seven years and was now, on a platform in Gaya, using it as the weapon it had always been.

Attention. The heels. The hands. The chin. The body's obedience to rank.

He spoke. He did not remember the words, the words had never been the point. The point was the speaking, the release of seven years.

"You are dismissed." The sergeant went. The platform was silent. The porters had stopped. The vendors had stopped. The crowd — he remembered the crowd. The crowd was already watching. They had been watching when he arrived. They had been watching from the moment he walked along the platform with his samosas and his chai and his officer's uniform, because a platform in India in 1946 watched a brown man in a British uniform the way a theatre watches a stage, attention, and the attention had been there before the sergeant, waiting, the platform already an audience before the performance began.

Then the sound. Not the eruption, the memory did not give him an eruption. The memory gave him precision. The sound began with a single voice. A child's voice. A boy, perhaps eight, perhaps ten, standing near the chai-wallah's cart with bare feet on the platform. The boy's voice was high and clear and the word was

Shabash. One voice. Then another. Then the stamping, the applause, the roar, but the roar had a starting point and the starting point was a boy, a child, a voice that said the word before the adults said it, because children do not wait for permission to approve, and this child had seen what the platform had seen and had said the word that the platform would say and the saying had begun with him.

On the bench in his garden in Devon, the boy's voice was in his ears. The boy who had said the word his own sons had never said. The boy who was young enough to be his son and who had stood on a platform with bare feet, had seen an Indian officer make a British sergeant stand to attention and had said *Shabash* and the word had started everything.

The hills of Devon. The garden. The bench. The fork against the wall.

The memory settled. It did not release him. Memories at eighty-two do not release; they merely recede, pulling back like a tide that leaves the sand changed, darker, wet, and the memory receded and what it left was the boy's voice, which was high and clear and had been with him for fifty years and would be with him for the remaining months, the voice that said the word, the word that meant *well done*, the word that meant *I saw you*. The German on the road had said *please*. The boy on the platform had said *Shabash*. The enemy's courtesy and the stranger's praise.

On the bench he remained. The stone was cold through his trousers, the November cold, the stone having surrendered its summer warmth months ago. He could feel each vertebra against the wall. The cold and the stone and the boy's voice, all held in the body at once. Ruth came to call him in for lunch.

II

He ate everything on his plate. Soup, leek and potato, Ruth's recipe, the recipe simple and the simplicity a virtue. He ate the bread with the soup. He cleaned the bowl with the last piece of bread, the china surface emerging beneath the crust's circular motion.

Ruth cleared the table. He heard her at the sink, the water, the cloth, the sound of a bowl being washed and set on the draining board. Small sounds. The sounds of a kitchen after lunch on an October day in Devon, what they had instead of speech.

In the sitting room the television was off. The shelf held its books, novels Ruth had read, a medical reference he still consulted, two Colditz books he had never opened and that Ruth had bought and placed there in the years before the recording, when the books were the closest she could come to the rooms where her husband had lived. Their spines faced the room. He did not look at them. Simply there, like the line on his chest, a mark the world had made and the world had forgotten.

The afternoon passed. The light moved across the sitting room. He read his medical journal, the *Lancet*, the pages dense with research he could follow and procedures he could not perform, as the Bengali he no longer spoke was a memory of a language. Ruth knitted. The needles clicked, a steady rhythm, the rhythm of hands always occupied, first with numbers at the bank counter, then with children and a house and the daily occupation of a marriage in which the other pair of hands could not always be reached.

He dozed. The journal open on his chest, the reading glasses sliding down his nose, and the drowsing came in the afternoons now without announcement, the body claiming its rest the way a creditor claims a debt, non-negotiable. The drowsing was light, he could hear Ruth's needles, the clock, a car on the lane, the sounds arriving through the thin membrane between sleep and waking. He came back. The journal had not moved. The light had. Ten minutes, perhaps fifteen. The body's small theft, accomplished without his consent.

Through the window the garden was visible, the bench by the south wall, the turned soil of the beds, the stone walls holding the last of the afternoon light. Beyond the walls, the Devon hills. A flock of starlings crossed the sky in a formation that shifted and re-formed, the birds following rules he could not see, the pattern beautiful, mathematical and moving south with a purpose that was not his purpose and that he watched with the detached attention of someone whose purposes were now contained within four walls.

He looked up from the journal. She was across the room. The light from the window behind her made her hair translucent: grey, fine, the light passing through it. Her face was in profile. The jaw that Ashok had inherited. The concentration of a woman counting stitches.

He looked at her for a long time. She did not notice, or she noticed and did not show it. He looked at her and what he saw was the woman who had placed a cup of tea outside the consulting room door while he spoke into a machine about things he had never spoken about to her. The placing of the cup. He could not account for it in any vocabulary he knew. He looked at her and turned back to the journal.

Light left the room. Ruth rose and turned on the lamp, the lamp made the room a room and the garden beyond the window became dark and the dark was Devon dark, soft, without the edges of other darks he had known.

She made tea. He drank it. They watched the news, the television's light moving across their faces, the world arriving in the sitting room with its concerns, and the concerns were not their concerns. The news ended. She turned it off. He read.

She knitted. At nine she said: “Bed?” And he said: “Yes.” And they went to bed the way they had gone to bed for forty-six years. She first. The bathroom sounds, the tap and the light switch. Then him, the same sounds, the same sequence, and they lay in the dark in the bed they had shared since Wales, and Ruth’s hand found his forearm, and the forearm held the hand, and the hand held the forearm, and the dark held them both.

STILL

Chapter 35

I

The winter came. Not the winter of the castle — not the Saxon cold that descended through stone and settled in the bones and stayed from October to April like a tenant who had signed a lease. Devon winter was different. Mild, wet, the cold arriving as rain rather than frost, the air soft even when it was cold, the softness a condition of the landscape that extended to the weather and the weather to the days. The rain had a sound on the Devon slate that was different from rain on any other surface he had known — softer than rain on stone, quieter than rain on tin. The garden went dormant. The soil he had turned in April lay open and dark, the rain fell on it and the only tending the garden received now, the body that had turned the soil in April could not kneel in January.

Quiet, the decline. It did not announce itself with crisis or collapse. It was a series of small withdrawals, the walk to the village that became the walk to the end of the lane, the end of the lane that became the garden gate, the garden gate that became the kitchen door. The perimeter closing. The world contracting around him as the courtyard at Colditz had contracted, each day a reduction, except that this contraction was imposed by the body itself, by the path of least resistance, by the available energy, by what the ground will bear.

Still the newspaper. Still the *Lancet*. Still the shaving each morning with care and dressed with a precision that was its own architecture. The shirt. The cardigan. The shoes, he had stopped wearing the garden boots. The shoes were indoor shoes now, soft-soled, the shoes of someone who has accepted that the outdoors and the indoors have merged, that the house is the world and the world is the house.

His weight dropped. The kitchen tiles bore a path worn smooth between sink and stove and table, the groove her feet had made over twenty years. Ruth tracked the thinning with her eyes, the eyes of forty-six years of cooking and reading his body as he had once read patients', the thinning visible in the neck, the wrists, the place where the collar sat differently. She cooked what he would eat. Soups. Toast. The dal on Sundays: she made it now, not him, working from the recipe he had taught her years ago. She poured the oil into the pan, measured or approximate, he could not tell anymore, and when the surface shimmered she added the cumin seeds and stood at the stove, her wrists steady, her hands performing the sequence without thought. The seeds darkened and she added the turmeric and the smell rose. He watched her from the kitchen table. Her face in the steam. The slight movement of her shoulders as she stirred. His mother's hands, executing his mother's knowledge, in his wife's body, in a Devon kitchen, the recipe surviving what everything else had not.

He tasted it. "More cumin," he said. And she added more cumin. The salt was wrong. She corrected it. The dal became itself.

Inward now, the clinical gaze. It had always been there, the doctor's habit of self-observation, the fingers on the radial artery each morning, the counting of the pulse that had been a habit since the hunger strike and that now, fifty-four years later, produced numbers he could not ignore. Resting heart rate: sixty-two. Blood pressure by palpation: elevated, the bounding quality in the radial pulse suggesting systolic hypertension. The murmur: still grade two, still systolic, but louder this month, audible higher in the chest, the aortic valve losing its argument with calcium, as all aortic valves lose their argument with calcium if the body lasts long enough. He could hear it when he lay on his left side at night. A soft, high-frequency sound that was not supposed to be there. He did not mention it to Ruth. He did not mention it to his own GP, a younger man in Paignton who called him Dr Mazumdar and whose competence he assessed, by habit, each time they met. The murmur was his. The diagnosis was his. The prognosis was obvious — the kind he had been living with since the bunk in Colditz, since the forty-two, since the heart had learned to speak a language the rest of him could not.

Afternoons in the consulting room. The tape recorder on the desk. The medical journals. The photograph of his parents, his father in a dark jacket, his mother beside him in a white sari, the photograph taken in Gaya before the war, the faces young, the faces of people whose son had not yet left for London and whose son had not yet walked toward tanks, whose son had not yet starved himself in a castle and whose son had not yet lost them without knowing he had lost them. The photograph was old. The edges were soft. The faces were unchanged.

He read. The *Lancet* carried a paper on cardiac rehabilitation in elderly patients. He read it with the attention he gave all medical literature, the methodology, the sample size, the confidence intervals, and the reading was a habit the mind would not relinquish. He made notes in the margin. Green ink on white paper. The handwriting had changed — smaller, less certain, the letters not quite connecting, the tremor visible in the downstrokes. He could see the tremor in his own handwriting as he had once seen it in patients', the fine motor control degrading, the neural pathways losing their bandwidth. He made the notes anyway.

Some afternoons Ruth came to the door. Not to ask anything. Not to bring tea. Simply to stand in the doorway for a moment, her hand on the frame, looking at him at his desk. He could feel the looking. He did not turn around. She stood there, he sat there. The room held them separately and together, the doorway between them a frame, and after a moment she went away and the room was his again.

Beyond him now, the garden. Not entirely, he could still walk the paths, still inspect the beds, still bend to pull a weed if the weed was shallow-rooted and the bending was brief. But the turning and the planting and the sustained work were over. He stood at the kitchen door some mornings and looked at the garden, surveying territory he had once governed and that was now self-governing, the weeds advancing, the beds unshaped, the stone walls holding a garden that was becoming, slowly, less than a garden. Ruth offered to hire someone. He did not want someone in his garden. He did not say this. Ruth read the silence, by the set of the jaw, and the subject was not raised again.

Christmas. Ashok came with his wife and children. Kamal telephoned from London, the children loud in the background, his wife's voice calling them to order. The call was brief — Kamal's way, the economy of a man who had inherited his father's conviction that what mattered between people did not require many words. He asked how Mazumdar was. He said he was well. He asked about the garden. He said the garden was resting. Kamal said he would come in January, and Mazumdar said good, and the good was sufficient, and the silence beneath it was the family's silence, the silence that belonged to all of them now, not a failure but a climate they had learned to live in, the way you live in a house whose load-bearing wall you do not remove.

Ashok's children were in the sitting room. He could hear them, their voices high and quick, the urgency of children who have been in a car for three hours and who have found a room with a carpet and space. The sound of children in the house was a sound the house had not held in years, and the sound filled the rooms, changing the air, making the house temporarily a different house. He sat in his chair. The children moved around him and through him. Life, the future, was the thing that would continue after the mornings stopped, and the thing did not know this and did not need to know it.

Ruth made Christmas dinner. He ate everything.

II

February. The mornings were harder. The getting-up took longer. The negotiation between the body and the will, which had been conducted in the early mornings since the hunger strike (the will saying *rise* and the body saying *wait*) the negotiation now favoured the body. He lay in bed for minutes after waking, from a stillness that was new, a reluctance to leave the horizontal, the body's honest assessment of what the vertical would cost.

Ruth's hand was on his forearm. He did not know if she was awake. The hand was there, the same hand, the same forearm, the same gesture that had begun in a bed in Wales in 1950 and had continued through Essex, Devon and forty-six years of nights. The gesture was a word. The word was untranslatable. The word existed only in the language of the gesture and the language had only two speakers and neither of them had ever attempted to teach it to anyone else.

Rising. The sequence: turn, sit, pause, stand. The pause was longer this month. The knees protested more specifically. The left ankle, which had turned on a stone on the far side of the gate at Chartres fifty-three years ago, reported a weather system it did not approve of. He stood. The standing held.

In the kitchen. The kettle. The toast. The butter knife. The plate.

Ruth arrived. The dressing gown, the slippers, the uncombed hair. She was thinner too, the sympathy between their bodies, the marriage expressing itself in parallel decline. She made her tea. She sat.

They ate. He ate everything. The plate cleaned. The crust set down. The newspaper. He unfolded it. He folded it into quarters. The headlines were the headlines of a winter morning, politics and weather and the concerns of a country that was proceeding without his participation, as countries do, as the country beyond the walls of Colditz had proceeded, as India had proceeded while he stood at a window in Cardiff watching another woman's sheets dry in the Welsh rain.

He read. Ruth read something of her own, a magazine, a letter from Ashok. The morning sounds, the clock on the wall, the boiler's hum, the wind against the window, a bird he could not identify because the frequency was in the range the hearing had surrendered.

Warm now, the kitchen. The heating had come on and the radiator beneath the window was ticking as it expanded. The warmth moved through the room: edges first, then tiles. His slippers were warm. His slippers were on the warm tiles. Ruth's slippers were on the warm tiles. Between them the table held the newspaper, the crossword, the toast plates, the two cups, the butter dish, the small domestic debris of a morning in progress.

Outside, the rain had stopped. The garden was grey-green, the winter lawn saturated, the stone walls dark with moisture. A magpie was on the garden wall. One for sorrow, Ruth had told him years ago. The English superstition. He had looked at her and said nothing because he had his own superstitions, buried deeper, and they were not about magpies.

The clock struck nine. The striking was soft, a mantel clock, the mechanism old, the sound aged into the house itself, becoming part of it rather than a sound within it. He turned a page. Ruth filled in a clue. The pen scratched. The clock finished its striking and the kitchen absorbed the silence that followed.

Up from the newspaper. He looked at Ruth. She was reading. Her glasses were at the end of her nose. The *Telegraph's* crossword, she did it in pen, the confidence of commitment.

"Ruth." She looked up. He did not know what he was going to say. The saying was not planned. The name had arrived in his mouth the way Bengali arrived in dreams, from beneath, from the place where names live before the mind has decided what to do with them. The name was in his mouth and the rest was not.

She waited. Her eyes on his face. The waiting was patient, the patience of decades, the patience he had seen in her hands when they waited for him to finish a thought, to choose a word, to decide whether to speak.

He looked at her. The light from the window. Her face. The face he had seen across this table and across other tables for forty-six years, the face that had changed as his face had changed: slowly, daily, the changing invisible from the inside and visible only in photographs that showed what time had done while they were not watching.

"Nothing," he said. "Never mind." She nodded. She returned to her crossword. He returned to his newspaper. The kitchen held them. The morning held them. The house held them. The walls, the roof, the kitchen, the window: all of it containing them, indifferent, providing nothing but its own structure. The garden was visible beyond the glass: dormant, dark with rain.

III

A morning. Late autumn: November, perhaps, or early December. The distinction between one morning and the next had become, by this point, a distinction the body did not make. The body made other distinctions now. The distinction between cold and colder. Between the stiffness that could be walked through and the stiffness that could not. Between the breath that came easily and the breath that required attention, the lungs asking for a supervision they had never previously requested.

He rose. The sequence. Turn, sit, pause, stand. The longest pause yet. Ruth's breathing beside him — steady, the rhythm unchanged. His own breathing was irregular now, the cardiac arrhythmia, the murmur producing its own rhythm beneath. He had matched his breath to hers for forty-six years without knowing it. He stood. The standing held. The standing would hold until it didn't. He stood. She breathed. The room held them separately.

The bathroom. The shaving. The face, thinner again, the orbital hollows deeper, the skin fitting the skull more closely, the skull emerging. He shaved it with care.

Shirt. Cardigan. The posture checked in the mirror, still straight. Still the posture of a man who walked toward things that needed walking toward. The shoulders would hold the posture until the shoulders could not, and the could-not was the body's business, and the body would attend to it in its own time.

Kitchen. The same kitchen. The kettle, the toast, the butter, the newspaper. The sequence performed as it had been performed every morning, the body's liturgy. Ruth was not yet down.

Ruth came in. The dressing gown. The slippers on the tiles. She filled the kettle. She made her tea. She sat across from him.

The steam rose between them. The kitchen held the sound of the clock and the boiler and the rain that had begun outside, light rain, arriving rather than falling, the air thickening into water.

He buttered his toast. The knife moved across the bread. The butter spread, evenly, to every edge, the whole surface covered. Ruth watched. His hands performed the act. The hands were slower this month, the tremor present, the grip that suppressed it weaker, and the weakness was a fact he had learned to hold gently, the way you hold a bird that is weakening. He adjusted. The adjustment was automatic. A surgeon's hands adjust.

He ate his toast. He ate every crumb. The bread moved in its circle and the china appeared beneath and it was done. Ruth's breath caught as the plate cleared — held and released, the involuntary response of someone watching an act they have seen a thousand times. The Crack was there, beneath the surface of the morning, as it had been beneath every morning since Berlin.

"More toast?" Ruth said. "No. Thank you." He knew the walls of this house. He had lived in it for twenty years. The consulting room's walls were plaster and lathe, and plaster and lathe do not hold sound the way stone holds it, and the recording had not been quiet, his voice, speaking for the first time about things that had been silent for fifty years, had not been quiet. She would have heard fragments. Words, *Colditz*, perhaps. *Bose*. Arriving through the wall with the muffled imprecision of sound through solid material. Not the details. Not the inventory. But the tone, the tone of his voice when the voice reached certain places in the telling, the measured control fracturing, what lay beneath it surfacing, the tone would have carried. Tone carries through walls. The content does not. She would have heard the sound of a man reaching the limit of what he could say, and the sound would have stayed with her.

What she understood, he did not know. He knew only what he could see, the change in her watching, the name said differently, the gaze that lingered. The forearm held in the dark. The plate observed each morning. The precision of his dressing, his folding, his cleaning, observed now with attention that had not been there before, or had been there all along and was now visible to him.

He picked up the newspaper. He folded it into quarters. Ruth returned to her crossword. Her pen stopped. She looked across the table at his hands on the newspaper, the tremor visible in the paper's edge, a vibration that had not been there a year ago. Three seconds. He did not see her looking. She saw his hands. She picked up the pen.

The pen moved, the small scratch of ink on paper. Her hand was steady. His was not. He noticed this — the diagnostic reflex, irrepressible — that her handwriting had not changed in forty-six years while his had become the handwriting of another man. The clock on the wall. The rain on the garden. The morning sounds of a house in Devon in which two people sat at a table and did what they had done every morning for decades.

Outside, the stone walls darkened with rain. The bare branches of the apple tree held water in beads. Somewhere beneath the garden the rain found its way down through soil and stone, underground, invisible, toward a river that was not the Phalgu and not the rivers of France and not the Mulde below the castle but a Devon river, going where Devon rivers go — to the sea, to the estuary, to the place where the fresh water meets the salt and the two waters merge and the merging is not visible from the surface, the surface calm and grey, giving no sign of what is underneath.

The morning continued.

HISTORICAL NOTE

This novel is inspired by the life of Dr Birendranath Mazumdar (c.1914/15 — December 1997), the only Indian prisoner of war known to have been held at Oflag IV-C, Colditz Castle, during the Second World War.

The historical framework for this novel draws primarily on Ben Macintyre's Prisoners of the Castle *(Viking, 2022), the authoritative secondary account of Colditz and of Dr Mazumdar's time there. It also draws on P.R. Reid's* The Colditz Story *(1952) and* The Latter Days at Colditz *(1953), Airey Neave's* They Have Their Exits *(1953), records held at The National Archives at Kew (including MI5 file Z/240), and publicly available military and repatriation records. The Imperial War Museum holds an oral history recording by Dr Mazumdar (Sound Archive Recording 16245), which was not directly consulted by the author but informs Macintyre's account and, through it, this novel. The Imperial War Museum has not authorised, reviewed, or endorsed this work. Mr Macintyre has not participated in, reviewed, or endorsed this novel; any errors of fact or interpretation are the author's alone.*

The documented facts drawn upon in this book include Dr Mazumdar's Edinburgh medical training, his commission in the Royal Army Medical Corps, his capture near Boulogne in May 1940, his transfer through German camps before arriving at Oflag IV-C in September 1941, his summons to Berlin in 1941 and his meeting there with Subhas Chandra Bose, his refusal of a commission in the Indian Legion, the sixteen-day hunger strike he undertook at Colditz, his escape from Frontstalag 153 at Chartres in June 1943 with a Sikh soldier, his walk across occupied France to Switzerland, his return to England, his private medical practice, his marriage, and his oral history recording in 1996, approximately one year before his death in Devon in December 1997.

Where the record is silent — which is to say, in every interior thought, every private conversation, every emotional response, every marital and familial scene, and every moment of decision in this novel — the author has imagined. Dr Mazumdar's wife, his children, his brothers, his parents, his fellow prisoners, the MI5 officers who interrogated him, and the Germans who captured and held him appear in this book as fictional versions of themselves. Certain minor characters are composites, invented for narrative purposes, or amalgamated from multiple historical figures. Certain events have been compressed in time or reordered for narrative clarity. Where the living were likely to be identifiable, names have been altered to protect the privacy of descendants. Where the person was already part of the public historical record, the name has been retained.

Subhas Chandra Bose was real. His twelve hours in private conversation with Dr Mazumdar in Berlin in 1941 are a matter of record, as is Dr Mazumdar's refusal of the Indian Legion and his return to captivity afterward. The content of their conversation — the arguments, the admissions, the sandesh, the offer, the silence — is the author's imagining. Bose's documented political positions, his public speeches, and his decision to form the Indian Legion are a matter of public record; the intimate, private register he is given in this novel is fiction, and should not be read as a claim about the man, his beliefs, or his conduct beyond what the record establishes. The estate, family, and representatives of Netaji Subhas Chandra Bose did not participate in the writing of this book.

The fate of Sowar Dariao Singh, 2nd Royal Lancers (Gardner's Horse), who escaped with Mazumdar from Frontstalag 153 Chartres in June 1943 and walked 900 kilometres to Switzerland, is unknown. No post-war record of Singh has been found. He disappeared from the historical record after the war, as completely as the Phalgu disappears into the ground at Gaya. The man in this novel bears his name out of respect for his role in Dr Mazumdar's escape. Readers connected to his family who wish to contribute to the record or request correction are warmly invited to make contact.

All dialogue, interior thoughts, motivations, and characterisations throughout the novel are the author's invention and should not be understood as factual claims about any real person. Readers who identify factual errors or who have concerns about the depiction of any named person are invited to write to info@yoddhalabs.com; corrections will be considered for subsequent editions.

ACKNOWLEDGEMENTS

This novel would not exist without Dr Birendranath Mazumdar, whose voice survives in the Imperial War Museum's Sound Archive. I owe him the attempt, however imperfect, to tell a story he could not tell himself.

To my late father, who scribbled story ideas in the middle of the night even as brain cancer was taking him. He ran out of time. I did not. This book is for the stories he would have written.

To my mother, whose love has been the one constant in every version of my life. Everything I am begins with her.

To my sister, who gave me a loving childhood and was the first person to sit still and listen to my stories. She has been listening ever since.

To my wife, my fellow traveller through the worlds of war, espionage, and the spirit. She reads what I read, watches what I watch, and endures what I imagine.

To the Luthras, the Roettgens, and the Kumars — my family, my sister's family, and my wife's family — for loving me with all their hearts.

The historical record of Dr Mazumdar's extraordinary life survives in scattered form — in P.R. Reid's Colditz memoirs, Airey Neave's escape narratives, Ben Macintyre's *Prisoners of the Castle*, the files at the National Archives at Kew, and the Imperial War Museum's collections. I am indebted to all of these sources and to the researchers and historians who preserved what might otherwise have been lost. The Colditz Society's records confirmed details of daily life in the castle.

Any errors of fact are mine. Any failures of imagination are also mine. The man deserved better than both. Readers who identify errors are asked to write to info@yoddhalabs.com so the record can be improved in future editions.

ABOUT THE AUTHOR

Rajat K. Luthra grew up in New Delhi. He is an alumnus of the Gemological Institute of America and the Hunter Centre for Entrepreneurship at the University of Strathclyde, Scotland. He has spent two decades as an entrepreneur in the jewellery industry.

He grew up reading Eric Williams and Paul Brickhill and stacks of Commando comics, and spent years wondering why none of the escape stories he loved contained Indian faces — despite India having contributed the largest volunteer army in the history of warfare. That question became an obsession, the obsession became research, and the research became two novels.

The Indian at Colditz is his second book, following *The Twenty Four* (2026). He is the founder of Yoddha Labs, a storytelling studio dedicated to the untold stories of Indian civilisation. He lives in New Delhi with his family.

ABOUT YODDHA LABS

India has five thousand years of civilisational history — of warriors, philosophers, mathematicians, navigators, and seekers — and almost none of it has been told to the world through modern storytelling.

The West built its cultural influence through novels, films, and games that turned its history into myth and its myths into global entertainment. India's stories — equally vast, equally dramatic, equally human — remain largely untold in the formats that shape how the world understands itself.

Yoddha Labs exists to change that. Founded by Rajat K. Luthra, Yoddha Labs is a transmedia storytelling studio dedicated to the untold stories of Indian courage, sacrifice, and civilisational depth. Through literary fiction, films, games, and immersive experiences, the studio brings to life the warriors, thinkers, and seekers whose stories have shaped the subcontinent — and whose legacies the world has never heard.

The Twenty Four — the true story of twenty-four Indian pilots who flew for the RAF in World War II — was the studio's first publication. *The Indian at Colditz* is the second. There are thousands more stories where these came from. We intend to tell as many of them as possible.

yoddhalabs.com

SELECTED SOURCES

Macintyre, Ben. *Prisoners of the Castle: An Epic Story of Survival and Escape from Colditz, the Nazis' Fortress Prison.* Crown, 2022.

Reid, P.R. *The Colditz Story.* Hodder & Stoughton, 1952.

Reid, P.R. *The Latter Days at Colditz.* Hodder & Stoughton, 1953.

Neave, Airey. *They Have Their Exits.* Hodder & Stoughton, 1953.

Imperial War Museum. Sound Archive, Recording 16245. Oral history of Dr Birendranath Mazumdar, c.1996. (Primary source for Macintyre's account; not directly consulted by the author.)

The National Archives, Kew. Military personnel records, POW camp records, and MI5 files relating to Indian subversion (file Z/240).

Commonwealth War Graves Commission. www.cwgc.org.

The Colditz Society. Historical records and documentation of Oflag IV-C.

FOR CORRESPONDENCE

Yoddha Labs welcomes correspondence from readers.

For corrections and queries regarding the historical record, concerns about the depiction of any named person, rights and permissions, press and review copies, or any other enquiry, please write to info@yoddhalabs.com.

Any complaint regarding the content of this novel will be considered on receipt. Factual corrections will be incorporated into subsequent editions; concerns about the depiction of named persons will be reviewed and, where appropriate, the text revised.

yoddhalabs.com

www.ingramcontent.com/pod-product-compliance
Lightning Source LLC
Chambersburg PA
CBHW050013170726
48282CB00025B/387
* 9 7 8 8 1 6 8 5 8 0 6 9 5 *